2 Tablets FOR YOUR Marriage

The 10 Commandments Applied To Marriage

Dr. TONY HART
author of "Winning is Everything"

2 Tablets FOR YOUR Marriage

The 10 Commandments Applied To Marriage

2 TABLETS FOR YOUR MARRIAGE:
THE 10 COMMANDMENTS APPLIED TO MARRIAGE
By: Tony Hart
Copyright © 2013
GOSPEL FOLIO PRESS
All Rights Reserved

Published by
GOSPEL FOLIO PRESS
304 Killaly St. W.
Port Colborne, ON L3K 6A6
CANADA

ISBN: 9781927521366

Cover design by Danielle Elzinga

All Scripture quotations from the
New King James Version unless otherwise noted.

Printed in USA

Dedication

I dedicate this book to my dear wife Carol who has taught me more about marriage and the application of God's law than all the books I have read on the subject. I owe so much to her and this book is the result of her instruction to me over 35 years. It is in the context of loving and failing that I have come to realize the relevant application of the commandments to marriage. Carol, thank you for the demonstration of these principles in your life.

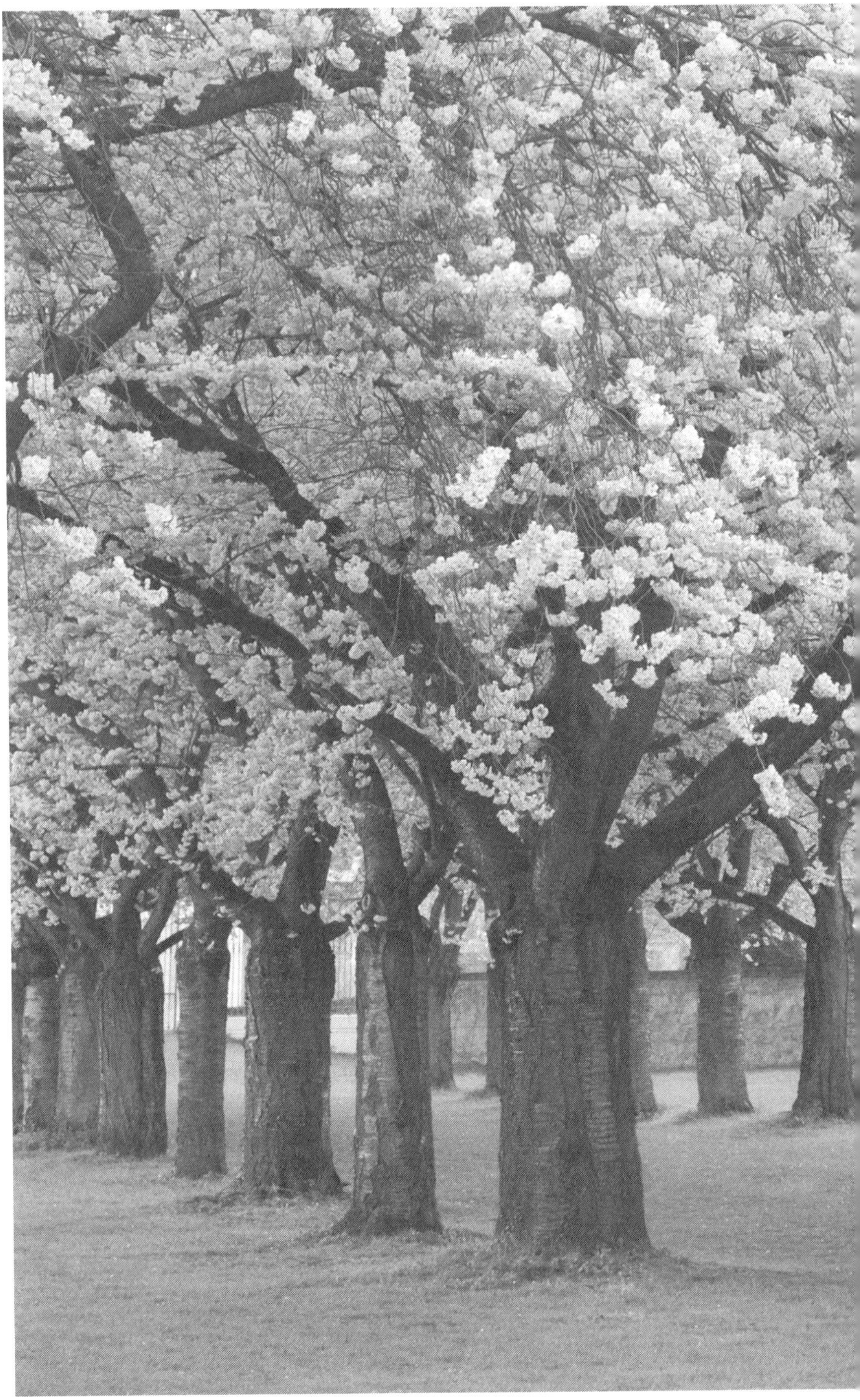

Introduction

Marriage has become a hot topic in our country. At the same time it is no longer considered sacred. Among Christians and non-Christians alike the marriage commitment has come to mean very little. In fact the divorce rate among those who claim to be born again Christians has almost caught up with that of the world. The problem is that we have not only forgotten the theological significance of marriage, but we have also forgotten the biblical foundation on which to build a healthy marriage. How is marriage to fulfill its God-given purpose in the context of a culture which does not support the institution of marriage, much less the biblical foundation on which a godly marriage is built?

As I study the Bible I am struck with the reality that **the moral law of God is fundamental to fulfillment in every area of life, especially marriage.** There is a blessing that flows back to us as we obey God's moral laws as spelled out in the Ten Commandments. This blessing is applicable to every relationship in our lives. However, since the marriage relationship is so central to many of us, it is particularly important to apply the moral law as found in the Ten Commandments to our marriages.

Throughout the Scriptures we find the Law of God being described as the source of an abundant life. In Deuteronomy 27:3, the Lord, speaking through Moses, challenged the people to teach and practice the Law of the Lord so that they would experience the abundant life in the land that God was leading them to. Some understand this as referring to the covenant spelled out in Deuteronomy 26:17-18. Others consider it to be pointing to the whole book of Deuteronomy. I suggest that this monument of whitewashed lime described in the next chapter would not have been large enough to contain the whole book. Moses was instructed to write on those stones *"all the words of this law"* (Deut. 27:8). The law that is referred to should be easily understood as the Ten Commandments given to Moses which stand as a summary of the unchanging moral Law of the Lord. It is this moral standard of God which, if obeyed, would bring praise and honour to the nation.

David instructed Solomon in 1 Kings 2:3, before he died, to keep all that is written in the law so that he would prosper in everything that he did. This represented David's dying advice to his son Solomon. Understanding that there is this connection between keeping the moral laws of God and prospering in your life, David reiterated to his son the same advice that Moses and the elders of Israel gave to the people as they prepared to enter the promised land (Deut. 27). In this passage David seems to expand his exhortation to include all of the statutes, judgments, and testimonies, provided by the entire written Scripture which was available to them at the time. This, however, in no way waters down or minimizes the effect of the promise that the Ten Commandments provide the basis for God's favour in our relationships.

The Bible says that the good hand of the Lord was upon Ezra because he set his heart to seek the Law of the Lord, and to do it, and to teach it (Ezra 7:9-10). I am encouraged by this Scripture. If we accept that the Commandments of the Lord are the basis for prosperity and good success in life, we are still left with discouragement and hopelessness since not one of us is able to comply with the stringent requirements of the law. The fact is that Ezra did not live up to the law as none of us do. The Bible makes it plain, in both the Old and New Testaments, that none are righteous and all have sinned and fallen short of God's standard.

As we read the passage, however, we note that God accepted a believing and willing heart that was both respecting the law and also taking advantage of the sacrificial provision for the shortcomings. The heart condition of Ezra was credited to him as righteousness and was found pleasing to God. 1 Samuel 16:7 makes it clear that while man looks on the outward appearance, God is looking at our heart. We can be encouraged then as by faith we join Abraham and Ezra and all those who have placed their faith in the provision for sin that God has provided for mankind. We are given position in Christ which makes it

Introduction

possible to receive God's blessings even as we journey by sanctification to comply with the law in our lives.

Psalm 1 reminds us that in order to be like a tree planted by the rivers of water we must delight in and meditate on the Law of the Lord. This instructs us that our hearts can be set on the Law of the Lord through meditation and delight. The process of constant meditation helps us to grow roots which will result in a stable delight and love for God. It will give us a firm foundation on which to build relationships which will not be shaken by every harsh circumstance. I have seen couples that have had their relationships dissolved over relatively minor issues simply because there was no root embedded in the moral laws of God.

This habit of meditation will follow only a true and heartfelt delight in God's law. We will never spend the time to think through the application of God's law to our lives unless we learn to value the law and to recognize that it provides the only pathway to pleasing God. Just because we do not possess the ability to perfectly keep the law does not mean that we do not value the law. It is that very appreciation for the need of God's righteousness that drives us to the foot of the cross and compels us to accept the righteousness that is offered through Christ. We must learn to appreciate God's standard of righteousness before we will even come to the cross in repentance.

In Psalm 19:7-11 we find David's appraisal of the value of the law to our lives. While the ceremonial law is no longer needed, the moral law summarized by the Ten Commandments is still valuable as a light to our path today. It is also a firm soil on which to build a relationship both with God and with others. That is why David wrote that the law is to be desired more than gold, even the finest gold. It is sweeter to the believer than honey, even the sweetest honey that comes right out of the honeycomb. If we can learn to appreciate the Law of the Lord as David did, we will delight in and meditate on it until our hearts are firmly planted in it like a tree planted by the rivers of water.

Marriage is symbolic of our relationship with God which is governed by the fulfillment of the law in Christ. **Our relationship with God is made more intimate by the process of**

conforming our lives to God's law. The process of sanctification is the process of making us look more like Christ. While the process may not always take us in a straight line toward Christ-likeness, and there may be detours and setbacks in our progress which at times have us moving in the wrong direction, in the long run there should be progress made in conforming us to the moral Law of God. In the same way, the relationship between husbands and wives is also made better by the application of God's law in the marriage. These laws are good for every relationship, but especially for the primary relationship found in marriage.

Marriage then is a reflection of our relationship with God as it portrays the love between Christ and the church. We literally paint a picture for the world to see. We present a demonstration of what the love between Christ and the Church looks like as we expose them to a marriage that applies the moral law of God to the relationship. This is an awesome responsibility and is God's purpose for marriage.

This theological understanding of the institution of marriage is carried out today in the context of a fast changing world with new cultural challenges. Many of these cultural factors hinder us from becoming one. A new mobility in our society has created a new set of challenges to marriage in the past several decades. In 1870 a thirty mile trip was an important event. Today many travel that far to shop or to work. At the turn of the nineteenth century we lived in ethnic groups which created islands of homogenous neighbourhoods. If I had been married in those days, my wife would no doubt have been someone who grew up within ten miles of me and who shared the same culture and values that I grew up with. Today, many marriages have to make major cultural adjustments that threaten the unity that God intended to demonstrate through marriage (Meredith, p. 30).

At the turn of the nineteenth century the home was the centre of most all activities. Recreation, education, religious study, vocational preparation, and emotional development were all focused in the home. When there was work to do

Introduction

everyone did their part, and when it was time to play, everyone participated (Meredith, p. 30-31).

Today, activities outside the home are the way of life. Each child has his own schedule and goes his own way. Even at home, the television has taken over and creative thinking, group interaction, and family discussions have been largely replaced. The spiritual and cultural ramifications of these changes are still to be fully discovered for generations to come.

Another major factor in marriage in recent decades is the change in the way we view marriage. One hundred years ago marriage was seen primarily as a practical issue. Physical strength and character were essential. Appearance was certainly considered but it was tempered by the practical considerations of running a farm. Survival back then for a woman who had been abandoned was very difficult and so she would have thought long and hard before marrying an unstable man. A strong back and courage were more important for success and the protection of the family. Sexual attraction was important but it was overshadowed by the more practical realities of life. Married life was seen through the lens of this practicality rather than the idealistic view of marriage as the road to emotional happiness (Meredith, p. 31-32).

Today, marriage is seen as essentially a social consideration. Social status and prestige are behind many marriages entered into over the last few decades. Very few couples enter into marriage for reasons of survival (Meredith, p. 36).

With this theological basis in place and understanding the changing cultural context in which we live, let's begin a journey of meditating on and applying to marriage the moral laws of God as presented in the Ten Commandments.

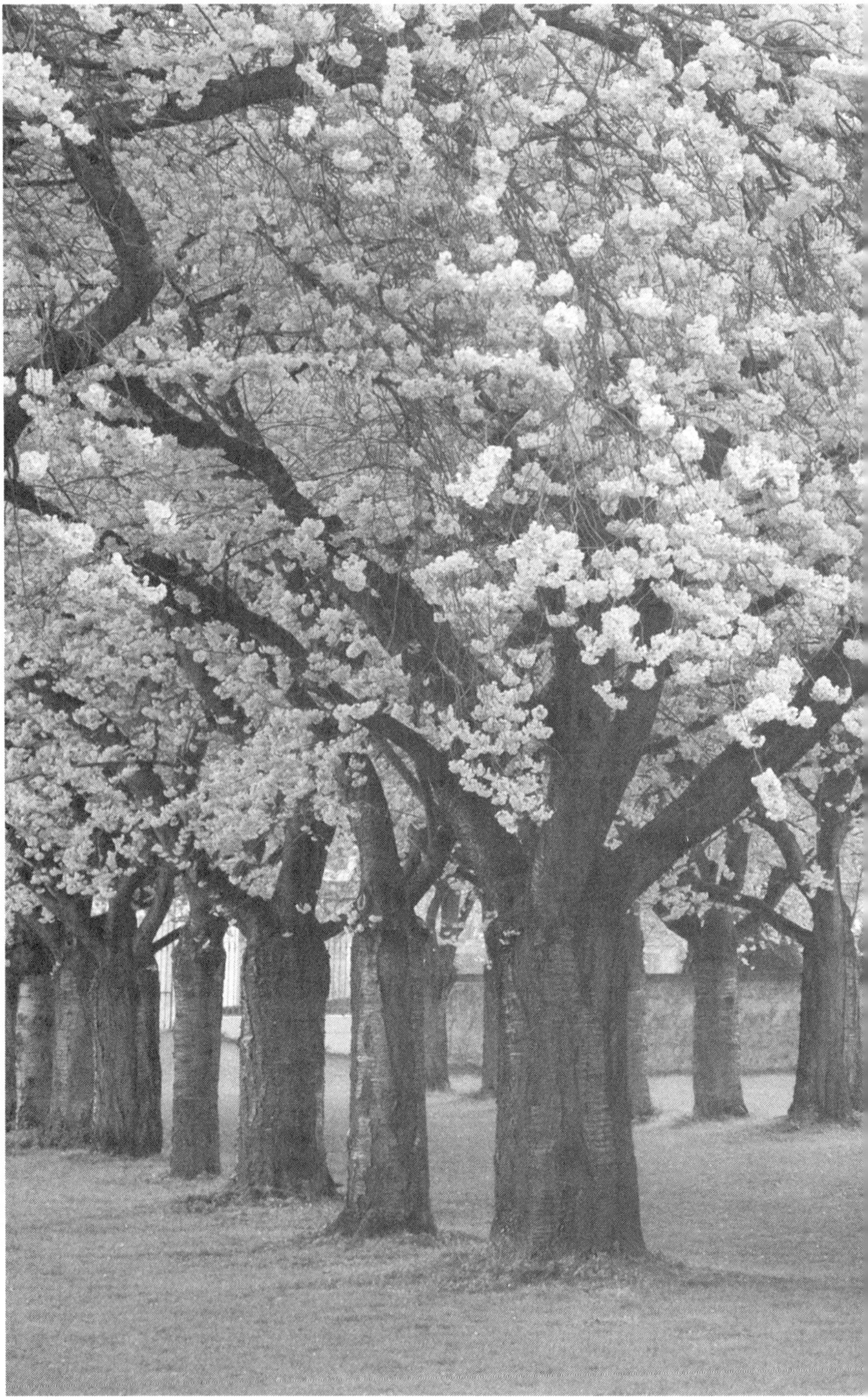

COMMANDMENT 1

"You shall have no other gods before Me"
Deuteronomy 5:7

Love the Lord with all of your heart.

In this first law which Jesus considered to be the Great Commandment, **we are commanded to make sure that God is always in first place.** If you love something or someone more than you love God, then your worship of that thing or person is idolatry.

We tend to think of idolatry as pagan worship of a statue God. The fact is that whenever there is something or someone that we love more than we love the Lord, we are committing idolatry and breaking this commandment. The rule is to love the Lord with all your heart. It is important to understand that we are finite human beings with a limited capacity to love. When our hearts are filled with anger, bitterness, even love for other things and people, it limits the capacity that we have to love God.

The dilemma is that we are commanded to love others. That includes our family, our neighbours, and even our enemies. Given the human limitations we are faced with, there is a problem complying with this first and greatest command to love the Lord with all of our heart. We all fall short right here at the very first commandment. None of us always loves the Lord first and foremost. We find ourselves with divided, even conflicting affections.

The way to have relative success with this command is to focus on the Lord giving special attention to the love and blessings that God has extended to us. When we allow the love of God to be prominent in our hearts, it will spill over to our other relationships, including our spouse. Therefore the love for my spouse should be an outgrowth of my love for God and not in competition with it. The love in my heart for my neighbour is part of my love and worship of God. It is therefore not based on their merit, but it is grounded in God's merit of my worship and devotion.

Be careful that you don't get sidetracked. Careers, money, possessions, and even our spouses and children can easily become the prominent loves that drive our lives. This is why it is important to draw a triangle and place God at the top of the triangle and ourselves and our spouse at the two bottom corners. Too often we spend our time trying to fix what is wrong

Love the Lord with all of your heart.

at the bottom of the triangle between the two parties. The fact is that if our focus and effort is primarily toward our spouse we will fail to find the satisfaction we desire. On the other hand, if we both pursue our relationship with God at the top of the triangle, then elementary geometry demonstrates how we will become closer together as we grow closer to God. The pursuit of God and His holiness in our lives is the only way to experience the oneness for which marriage was created. To the extent that our hearts are filled with love for the Lord, we will comply with the design of this first law and see its benefits in the oneness that God has designed for our marriages.

The game of Monopoly illustrates how we get sidetracked with things that don't matter. My family loves to play Monopoly when we go on vacation. Everyone around the table is busy making deals, accumulating property, and collecting rent from houses and hotels. The intensity of the game reaches a peak when the strongest player with the most property puts everyone else out of the game. The fact to note here is that, after the game is won, all the houses, hotels, deeds, railroads, and utilities all go back in the box until the next time the family all gets together. That is so much like our lives. We get so caught up with the pursuit of possessions and power but when this life is over we can't take any of it with us.

My challenge to you then is to make sure that God stays as the first priority in your life. He should be the centre of your attention and joy. Until you are willing to put God before even mother or father, your sister or brother, yes even your husband or wife, you will be trapped in the futility of idolatry according to Matthew 10:37. As long as we are expending all our energy **at the bottom of the triangle we will miss the oneness that marriage aspires to.** Date night and vacations can't produce the oneness that having God in first place, filling our hearts, can produce. The best thing that we can do for our marriages is to commit to having God first in our lives and loving Him with all our hearts.

When God comes first, then what we do for our spouse becomes part of our service to God. Our love is not a reward for good behaviour, or tit for tat, as though we were entering into or executing a contract. We husbands are to love our wives because we love God, and we desire to please Him, and He commands us to love our wives. Wives are to respect their husbands because they respect God and desire to please God by fulfilling this Great Commandment.

We may think that this is all optional for a believer, but 1 John 3:10 tells us that whoever does not love his brother is not of God. In other words, one of the characteristics of a true believer is that he is able to love his brothers and sisters in Christ, even those who are unlikeable. Jesus makes a stronger statement when He tells us in Matthew 5:44 to love our enemies and pray for those who would despitefully use us. Husbands and wives need to consider their spouses to be more than just another brother. Your spouse may feel like your enemy at times, but for most of us it is simply selfish idolatry which refuses to put God first and accept the assignment of loving our spouses. If you love God, then you will seek to keep His commandments.

The problem begins when we care more about our feelings than we do about our relationship with God. This commandment is all about putting God first, ahead of all others and even ahead of our own emotions. Following our emotions will lead us into a desire for satisfaction from revenge, payback and malice. When two people put God in first place, however, you have the makings of a powerful union. As they draw closer to the top of the triangle, they increasingly experience the oneness that God designed for the marriage relationship. All other relationships and interests are brought under the control of the regulating love of God shed abroad in our hearts.

That is why before you get married, you need to be sure that your spouse is headed in the same direction. When marriage becomes about happiness, or financial security, or children, then you will never fulfill this commandment. Your marriage has to be about fulfilling God's purposes and not your own. Marriage at its foundation is about filling the earth with the image of God. Unity in marriage is experienced when we conform our lives to His image, encourage our spouse to journey with us, and meet at the top of the triangle. It is only

Love the Lord with all of your heart.

then that we will demonstrate the oneness that God gives as the goal for each godly couple.

In order to find the unity at the top of the triangle however, we are to make sure that the person we are marrying is also pursuing a relationship with God. So many people are getting married for other reasons. It is essential that you do your homework and watch the life of that prospective husband or wife, as well as check your own heart for other motivations. When the Apostle Paul wrote *"be not unequally yoked together with unbelievers,"* he did not mean to make sure that the guy goes to church, or was baptized. We are to examine the life of that prospective mate and make sure that moving to the top of the triangle is a top priority for that person. There have been many disappointed spouses who married a person who went to church but who didn't love God and was not exhibiting the priority of an intimate relationship with God.

Ginie Sayles conducts a course called "How to Marry the Rich." The four-hour class focuses on how to find a rich mate and how to get that wealthy prospect to the altar. As far as finding wealthy single people, the teacher advises looking at charity events or art classes. And if at first you don't succeed, Sayles counsels you to keep trying. The idea is to date anybody who is sane and breathing as long as they are rich (*Emphasis*, Sept/Oct, 2001, p. 15). The priority for many may be money, but the priority for the believer who loves God should be to find a mate who loves the Lord and places Him in first place in his life. I would suggest then that you replace the priority of money and good looks with the priority of love for God.

If the world can place such blatant emphasis on monetary qualifications then we as believers need to be equally unwavering in our search for someone who loves God first and with all their heart. It is important that both husband and wife desire to please the Lord and to love Him above all else. If you are already married and God is not the priority in your spouse's life then your prayer needs to be focused on that heart issue. It will do little good to spend a lot of money and time in secular counseling about communication, money, and child-rearing, while ignoring the central issue of the heart toward God. Those other things certainly have their place but the real oneness that God desires for all of us in our marriages will not be realized until both parties are placing their respective relationships with God at the top of the triangle as the priority in their lives.

Love for our spouse can be easily supplanted by seemingly greener pastures. We need to understand how we can maintain our love for the Lord and how to refuel our love along the long journey till death do us part. We find three refueling stations in Matthew 7:1-29. The first stop which helps us to refuel our love reminds us to take a good look at the plank in our eyes. We often spend so much time going over the faults of our spouses and rehearsing them to ourselves as well as to them. Meanwhile, while our focus is on the shortcomings of the other person, we lose track of the fact that we are carrying a boulder worth of sin in our own lives. It is at this first stop that we remember our own sins and become more patient and forgiving with others. In the Sermon on the Mount, Jesus reminds us that malice and bitterness will block our worship. So we are told to reconcile those relationships and then return to our worship with a heart cleared of ill will and critical thoughts so that we can fill our hearts with love for God.

The second stop at our refueling station is found in the picture of our lives as a tree which bears fruit. The result of stopping at this tree confirms the conclusion that the problem in us is not the fruit or outward manifestations of sin, but the real problem in our lives is a problem of a lack of love for God and others in our hearts. We often think that different circumstances, maybe a different partner, or a different financial status, would change our relationships. The fact is that we need to keep in mind that the real problem is in our hearts. So these first two stations simply tell us that we are just as messed up as our partner, and that the problem is much deeper than it looks on the outside. As much improvement as I think that my wife needs to make, I am reminded here that I am no better. In fact, I am the chief of sinners and her sin is no worse than mine. I am challenged to deal with my heart issues before tackling

Love the Lord with all of your heart.

hers. The reality is that my heart change will be the challenge of a lifetime leaving me little time to focus on her issues.

I spoke to a wife not long ago who was troubled at her husband's lack of communication and apparent ingratitude. So after talking about how she would like to see her husband change, I asked her how she thought the Lord would like to see her change. Was God allowing this trial in her life to work out any change in her? As you can imagine, she saw no problem that needed any change in her life; the problem was her husband. This woman needs to visit these first two stations before she can reload any love for her husband.

The third and last refueling station given to us in this text is a visit to the cross to remember what Jesus has done for us. Our fulfillment of the Great Commandment to put love for God in first place and to love others as we love ourselves is possible only as we come to this third station. It is at the foot of the cross that we can take a fresh look at the incredible love that God demonstrated for us in spite of our sin. While we were stuck in our sin without any hope, Christ died for us. He didn't withhold any of Himself because we were rebellious. He didn't limit his willingness to sacrifice his life in order to provide us with the salvation that comes only through Jesus Christ. As we pause in our busy lives to periodically take a fresh look at what happened there at Calvary and the love that was demonstrated for us, we experience a renewal of the love of God being shed abroad in our hearts. It is simply the overflow of that love for God in our hearts that gets directed to the others around us. How can I withhold love from my admittedly sinful spouse when God so immensely loves the awful sinner that I am.

The communion we have around the Lord's table becomes an opportunity for us to visit all three of these stations. It enables us to refocus our hearts and renew our love for God. If anything in our hearts hinders us from complying with this first commandment, a visit to the third station of Calvary will provide the victory.

It is interesting that, in the text, the third station is described as a rock on which a wise man builds his house (Matt. 7:24).

The cross work of Christ at Calvary is to be considered the only foundation rock on which our lives can be built. Any other foundation on which to build your life or your marriage is to build your house on sinking sand.

The outward manifestation of building on the Rock of Christ is our obedience to Christ. John says that if you love God you will obey Him. In other words, the fruit which grows from a heart filled with love for God is the fruit of obedience. Don't tell me that you love God and that He is in first place at the top of your triangle and then turn around with excuses as to why you can't obey him. No wonder Jesus taught that the fulfillment of this Great Commandment is the fulfillment of the entire law.

Application Questions

1. Where in our relationship has God not been first?
2. How can we help each other to keep God in first place?
3. Spend time together in prayer.

COMMANDMENT 2

"You shall not make for yourself a carved image—any likeness of anything that is in heaven above, or that is in the earth beneath... you shall not bow down to them nor serve them."

Deuteronomy 5:8-9

Don't allow for any idols in your life.

2 Tablets for Your Marriage

A woman ordered a mink stole through a catalogue sales company. When she got home after an afternoon of shopping she saw her husband lying unconscious by the mailbox. There beside him was a package. "Oh goodie," the woman shouted, "It's here! It's here!" She then literally stepped over her unconscious husband in order to grab the package that she had been waiting for.

There are some things that have become far too important to us. Money, children, homes, even our marriages have consumed our hearts. Anything that competes with our love for God can become an idol. Idolatry is not limited to replacing the worship of the true God with another religious form of worship. Most of us as Christians recognize the fact that money and possessions can become idols and so we try to check ourselves and make sure that we are not too consumed by the desire for these things.

Most Christians however are not aware of the insidious fact that **happiness has become the number one idol in our culture today.** Our theology has even caused many Christians to ask when faced with trials in life, "Doesn't God want me to be happy?" Unfortunately, many have justified leaving marriages, jobs, and other relationships under this false theology that places happiness at the top of the triangle. We have falsely justified many bad decisions believing that God's priority is to make us happy.

The reality is that happiness is fleeting; it is like a vapour. We grasp for it and just when, for a moment, we think we have it, it's gone. The confusion stems from our inability to distinguish between the joy that God desires for us to experience and the happiness that the world offers. Happiness is a response to the circumstances of our lives. Therefore it is fleeting and cannot be sustained through the trials of life. I have defined the joy of the Lord as **a supernatural, deeply rooted, sense of fulfillment that comes when we know that we are where God has called us to be and are doing what God has given us to do.** According to James McDonald, joy grows out of an appreciation for the person of God, the purpose of God, and the people of God. It is not based on circumstances and so we say that the world didn't give joy to you and the world can't take joy away.

Don't allow for any idols in your life.

The Apostle Paul is a good example. Imagine if he had lived in our day with our view of entitlement to a happy life. As he journeyed on his mission trips he was stoned, left for dead, and persecuted. We would have counseled him that this could not be God's will for his life. After all, doesn't God want you to be happy. Paul was not "happy" as the stones were beating him on his head. There is no way he was feeling happy lying there in pain and suffering persecution. I believe that through all of the persecution Paul experienced the joy of the Lord. He had that supernatural, deeply rooted, sense of fulfillment that comes when you know that you are doing what God has called you to do and where God has placed you. Paul was able to write to the Philippian church and tell them to rejoice, or in other words, to experience the joy of the Lord in all things.

There have been times when I have complimented my wife on how pretty she looks. Often her response is to say that her hair is a mess, or her old dress wasn't so pretty. I have to remind her that when it comes to her beauty, her hair didn't give it to her and her hair can't take it away. As Christians we also need to remember that when it comes to the joy of the Lord, it doesn't come from the situation that we are in but rather is a supernatural, deeply rooted sense of fulfillment that only God can give.

Whether we struggle with the idol of happiness, or some other form of idolatry as the driving force in our lives, we need to come clean with God and get rid of all our idols. Surrender all of our idols as we present our bodies a living sacrifice to God.

We all create images on the blank video that we are born with. We develop a picture in our heads of what we believe life should resemble. If you ask a toddler what he or she wants to be when he grows up you may get an answer such as a policeman or a nurse. When that same child becomes a teenager and you ask them what their life will look like, they have developed a more sophisticated picture of Mr. Tall-dark-and-handsome, a house on the hill with a long driveway and 2.5 well behaved children. Now check in with that same person during his middle ages and you find frustration and often resentment because life rarely turns out the way you dreamed it to be. Mr.

Tall-dark-and-handsome is short, bald and poor. The hardest thing for us to do is to hit the eject button in our heads and hand the DVD with all our dreams and desires over to God. In the words of Romans 12:1-2 present it all to God as a living sacrifice and allow Him to rewrite and record all His plans for you. As we become willing to give up the idolatry of pursuing our own goals and aspirations we will then begin to experience the good and acceptable will of God. Give it all to God and let him erase all those idols and renew your mind. This second commandment requires us to constantly search our hearts and make sure that there is nothing competing against God. No plans, no desires, no love, can be allowed to replace that top spot in our hearts that God desires to hold. It is only then that we will experience the joy of the Lord.

Idolatry will ruin your marriage. Patrick Morley defines an idol as something other than God that you believe will make you happy. Our marriage mirrors our love for God. If our love for God is easily taken out of its place by idols, then our love for our spouses will be easily moved out of our hearts. We worship, value, and love so many things more than we love God. ie.— family, money, comfort, happiness. All these become threats not only to our relationship with God, but also to our intimacy in marriage with our spouse. When someone tells me that they have fallen out of love with their spouse I can show you someone who has fallen out of love with God, someone who has allowed their heart to become clogged with idols.

Idolatry also will cause your priority wheel to be out of balance. When our priorities are out of line with God's purposes, life turns into a state of disarray. The whole area of understanding priorities has gone through a bit of a revolution in my mind. One day as I was thinking about the vertical view of priorities I had been raised with, it struck me that the vertical model was not very helpful. I was taught that our priorities should be listed as God first, family second, and ministry third. This model left me frustrated and offered little help in making day-to-day decisions.

For when could I ever say that I was finished with God so as to go to the next priority of family. Likewise, when could I ever

Don't allow for any idols in your life.

say that I was finished with family so that I could move to the next priority of ministry. The vertical list of the priorities doesn't help with those decisions of moving down the list and allocating your time. I began to realize that maybe a more helpful view of the priorities in life was the model of a wheel. God is the hub and the centre of the wheel and coming out from the hub are the spokes of various responsibilities which God has given to each of us.

The conviction that I bring to this model is that God is sovereign. Alongside this understanding is the promise that God will not place more on us than we can bear. With these two anchors firmly in place I can approach life with the confidence that I can succeed with all of the spokes of responsibility placed in my wheel. My responsibility then is to take care of each responsibility which God places in my life. That means that there are some times when the family is in need of more of my time in order to get the wheel back in balance. There are other times when the ministry needs more of my time. The goal however remains the same. It is always to keep the wheel in balance as we progress on the road of life.

The vertical model has allowed many well meaning people to neglect their families because they have concluded that God comes before family. Likewise many have neglected ministry because this model has taught them that family comes before ministry. The priority wheel reminds us that we don't have the option to neglect any responsibility which the Lord has given to us. If you feel as though you have more responsibilities than you can bear, then I suggest that you have added a few spokes to your wheel that God didn't give you. God does not give us more than we can handle. Many of us need to examine our lives and ask ourselves what is it that we have added to our wheel that God did not put there. Often those extra spokes represent idols in our hearts which hinder our ability to obey God. So a man who spends a day each week with his hobby or sport will turn down using his gifts in ministry and use the excuse that he needs to spend time with his family. Remember, if we love Him, we will obey Him and fulfill all that He requires of us. That will require setting aside all idols and rooting out the love for them from our hearts.

Application Questions

1. What idols have thrown your life out of balance?
2. Can you give every area of your life to God?
3. What is it that you believe will make you happy?
4. Ask your spouse to help you identify those things that have become more important than pleasing God.

COMMANDMENT 3

"You shall not take the name of the Lord your God in vain."
Deuteronomy 5:11

You shall guard the name of the Lord.

I have had the experience of walking into a room or workplace and being exposed to the disrespectful use of the Lord's name. It should be repulsive to anyone who worships the Lord and desires to give Him His rightful place in our hearts. Most of us have at one time or another been offended by those who use the name of the Lord disrespectfully. To take His name in vain simply means to use it without the respect due to God. This goes beyond the obvious use of the Lord's name attached to cursing and swearing. When we use His name flippantly and without regard to the respect that He deserves we become guilty of violating this command.

If marriage is a picture of our relationship with God then we also need to guard the name of our spouses. (Eph. 5:25-27) The Lord doesn't have any stupid children, worthless bums for children. We are the bride of Christ and as the church we are still a work in progress. But despite all our imperfections, we are loved and treasured. The relationship that we have with Christ demands that we respect Him and guard His name while He loves us. In order to accurately reflect our relationship with the Lord, we are to also guard the name of our spouse. Our marriages are to be advertisements of the relationship that exists between Christ and the church. How we talk to and about each other goes a long way toward being the kind of billboard that we should be.

The most significant application is to protect the name and reputation of our spouses. We unfortunately live in a world which has made it politically correct to bash men and so many wives have fallen into the trap of talking negatively about their husbands to girl friends and family. The problem has existed for a much longer time with men putting down women. The "old ball and chain" or the "old lady at home" has been around for a long time. It may be socially acceptable to speak disrespectfully about your spouse but it should be just as repulsive to us as using the Lord's name in vain.

How you talk about God's children is a reflection of what you think about God. Wives before you join in with the male bashing, remember that your husband represents Christ.

You shall guard the name of the Lord.

Husbands, before you entertain critical thoughts toward your wife remember she is God's gift. It has been said many times that a problem with the gift is a reflection on the Giver.

In Matthew 25:45 Jesus said that inasmuch as you did it not to the least of these, you did it not to me. This is no less true when we are talking about how we speak to and about each other. God takes it personally how we treat each other. Imagine then that you are being that disrespectful to Jesus Himself. The reality of that truth should be enough to stop us in our tracks. There is no room for verbally putting down each other. If we love God and reflect that love by loving our spouse then stone throwing should never take place.

Applying this third commandment in your marriage means that **you promise to never throw stones.** People who live in glass houses don't throw stones. Some of us forget how fragile our glass houses are. If there is anyone who knows where all the glass is in our lives, it is our spouse, and so it makes no sense to begin a stone throwing fight with someone who knows so well how to hurt us.

Learning how to argue is an important skill that many people never learn. One important rule is to stay focused on the issue and to never allow the verbal exchange to disintegrate into name calling and personal attacks. Make a commitment to God and to your spouse today that from this day forward you will never again throw stones. Therefore rather than directing all your frustration into a verbal stone fight we should direct more of our energy toward the Lord in prayer concerning the relationship struggles that we face.

Encouragement is the opposite of verbally putting down. Encouragement is an important part of guarding the name of our spouse. There are some people that become known as encouragers. Even when there are things to criticize and correct, they are able to balance criticism with encouragement. Other people are always negative. There is always something wrong. The glass is always half empty. As the saying goes, you can gather more flies with honey than with vinegar. Likewise, encouragement is much more effective than criticism. This is true in dealing with our children as well as dealing with spouses, employees, church people, and casual relationships.

As the passengers settled in on a West Coast commuter flight the flight attendant announced, "We'd like you folks to help us welcome our new co-pilot. He'll be performing his first commercial landing for us today, so be sure to give him a big round of applause when we come to a stop." The plane made an extremely bumpy landing, bouncing hard two or three times before taxiing to a stop. Still, the passengers applauded. Then the attendant's voice came over the intercom, "Thanks for flying with us. And don't forget to let our co-pilot know which landing you liked best."

Like those passengers it would have been easy to point to the faults of the pilot. It takes no work to find something to criticize but the challenge is to be an encourager. Any married couple can tell you the things worthy of criticism. This commandment calls on us to reverence and respect our spouses so that we encourage rather than tear down.

Don't tear down but encourage growth. Promise today that you will never throw stones, but that you will be an encourager. Why is it that some people struggle with guarding? Throwing stones? Encouragement?

I am not suggesting that you stick your head in the sand when it comes to constructive criticism. It is an act of love to speak the truth and to point out areas where improvement is needed. When no one else will tell you the truth, a loving spouse can help by being painfully honest. The challenge is to speak the truth as an encourager. A good exercise is to try and balance every criticism with a compliment or encouragement. Try it, it is not that easy, but if you can pull it off you will quickly be known as an encourager even as you deal with the difficulties that have to be addressed in any relationship. This exercise applies to parents dealing with children as well as to any adult relationship.

This commandment to guard the name of your spouse requires the ability to forgive. Matthew 18 gives us an excellent picture of the dynamics of forgiveness. We find in this Scripture

You shall guard the name of the Lord.

that Peter comes to Jesus and asks Him how to continue to forgive someone who repeatedly commits the same offense. We can all relate to this dilemma. Imagine that a man walks by you and, without watching where he is going, steps on your foot. It is easy to offer forgiveness the first time, but then he walks by again and steps on your foot a second time. You can sense frustration building but, with a little exhortation to be careful in the future, you offer forgiveness again. Now imagine this same man comes by and steps on your toe a third, fourth, fifth time. Peter's question becomes very relevant. How many times am I supposed to forgive him? Can I finally retaliate after seven times? After all, isn't that the biblical number of completion?

Jesus answered and said, not seven times, but seventy times seven. If you do the math it equals 490 times. The point that Jesus was making was not that we should keep track but that we should continue to forgive without counting. He purposely used a high number that would be beyond our ability to easily keep track of. Except for Carol having to constantly tell me to put the toilet seat down when I use it, there are few offenses in our household which exceed the 490 number. So the problem shared by all of us with Peter is simply where do we find it in ourselves to continue to forgive when someone repeatedly offends us.

Jesus answers the question with a parable about an unforgiving servant (v. 23). There was a king who wanted to settle accounts with his servants by collecting the money that he had out on the streets. One particular servant was brought in who owed the king ten thousand talents. Jesus uses this large sum of money to make an important point. Ten thousand talents was more money than the Gross National Product of Israel at the time. In today's terms, He would have used billions of dollars as the debt of this servant. It was clearly more than this servant would ever see in his lifetime. There was no hope of ever being able to pay back this huge debt. After begging the king for time, even though more time would have been futile, the king had compassion on the servant and forgave him the entire debt.

Can you imagine the servant, elated, skipping out of the palace, completely free from the weight of the debt which hung over his head? He must have been anxious to go and tell his family the good news. A new lease on life had begun. Indeed he would have described to them a born again experience. Well, on his way out the palace he runs into an old friend who owed him a hundred denarii. This was no small sum. It represented about three months wages for the average worker of his day. If someone owes you three months wages you want your money. Jesus used a significant debt which was owed to the servant so that we don't dismiss as easy and insignificant the forgiveness which the story proposes. It was however a sum which could have been worked out with some kind of payment schedule. This servant didn't even want to work with his friend in resolving the debt; so he grabbed him by the throat and threw him into prison till he paid the whole sum.

Notice the response of the king. In verse 32 the king calls the servant in and chides him by reminding him, *"You wicked servant! I forgave you all that debt because you begged me."* This is the first step in finding it in our hearts to forgive those who repeatedly offend us. We must remember that we ourselves are the recipients of great forgiveness. Too many of us forget the huge pile of debt from sin that we have been forgiven.

The second step is in verse 33 where the servant is exhorted, *"Should you not also have had compassion on your fellow servant, just as I had pity on you?"* The fact for us to face here is that we are also unwilling to forgive even after we have been forgiven so much. The failure of the servant is our failure today. We allow ourselves to forget how much we have been forgiven and to live in a state of self-righteousness. No wonder we struggle to forgive others who offend us.

The place to go to be constantly reminded of our release from the bondage of our debt is the foot of the cross. No wonder Jesus invited us to join Him around the communion table to remember our time before the King. It is there at the foot of Calvary that we find what it takes to forgive those who transgress against us. Only then can we forgive even those who exceed the 490 threshold.

You shall guard the name of the Lord.

Ruth Bell Graham said, "A good marriage is between two forgivers." This is indeed a very critical skill which must be learned in order to experience the oneness of marriage. I have been asked, "What happens if only one is able to forgive?" The fact is that one is better than none although two is better than one. All we can do is to take care of ourselves and pray for our spouses.

One of the important lessons I have learned is that I am not entitled to forgiveness from others. So I can rejoice in the forgiveness from God and learn from the offenses that I create for others. As I learn and repent of sin in my life I can extend love and grace even to those who don't offer forgiveness to me.

Another question I am asked is whether I can forgive even if the other person does not apologize and ask for forgiveness. There have been two schools of thought on this matter. Some teach that you can forgive only after someone asks for forgiveness. The point is made that God forgives us only after we come to Him and ask in repentance. This approach places us in the position of God who knows no sin and is without transgression. God has no obligation to forgive and extends grace to us without any obligation to do so. We, on the other hand, are like the servant who has been forgiven a huge debt and should by obligation freely extent that grace to others without condition.

This parable involved a person who repeatedly offended without repentance or change. Once we start placing conditions on our forgiveness we end up in a quagmire of judging sincerity. I can't forgive him. Didn't you see that smirk on his face? I don't think he really meant it! All the while, being unwilling to forgive, we are held hostage to that person and damage only ourselves.

As we become proficient at forgiving as we have been forgiven, our hearts are cleared of malice and bitterness. We can then fill our hearts with love for that person which will result in respect reflected in how we speak to and about them. This third commandment demands that as we advertise our relationship with God to the world in marriage, we guard the name of our spouse as we would guard the name of the Lord.

2 Tablets for Your Marriage

Application Questions

1. What is it that you need to forgive your spouse for?
2. Tell your spouse that you are letting it go today.
3. Promise that you will be an encourager and not a stone thrower.
4. Promise to never speak badly to others about your spouse but to always guard his/her reputation.

COMMANDMENT 4

"Observe the Sabbath day, to keep it holy..."
Deuteronomy 5:12

Remember to save one day for the Lord.

The concept of the Sabbath goes back to creation. There are many today who want to limit to the Law of Moses this principle of one day out of seven. The creation account points out the existence of this Sabbath principle even before the law was given. It was reinforced in the Law of Moses and in the promises to God's people. The principle did not end with the coming of Christ. After the resurrection, Christians began to observe the first day of the week as the Lord's Day according to John 20. As believers we are still encouraged to Sabbath on the Lord's Day, not as a matter of legality, but to set aside time to worship and to develop our relationship with God. Our modern culture, after the post World War II years of the middle twentieth century, has made it difficult and has not supported Christians in the effort to maintain this important discipline. Christians work on Sundays and youth sports hold games on Sundays which conflict with the time that we would gather to worship. It takes strength and commitment to reserve that time for the Lord.

Your marriage should be a picture of the relationship between Christ and the church. **So as you commit to go to church on the Lord's Day, also commit to spend time each week with your spouse.** This application of the fourth commandment assumes that we are spending time working on our relationship with the Lord. It is only after the discipline of Sabbath time with God is being exercised that we can apply this in the same way to our spouses. If this is not the case in your life, then the first place to start is with a commitment to spending quality time with the Lord and with His people. It was pointed out in the first chapter that our love for our spouse is to be an outgrowth of our love for God. He is to be at the top of the triangle and at the hub of the wheel of our lives. Our marriage is only a picture or reflection of our relationship with God.

Dating should not end after the wedding. When time and money get tight, dating is the first thing that goes. I have been married a long time and I have fallen on and off of this wagon several times. I have learned through many mistakes that devoted time for my spouse is as important as it is difficult. As with any commitment, this requires us to say no to competing interests which will get in the way.

Remember to save one day for the Lord.

I remember a number of years ago during a time when I was briefly on the wagon, that I was pressed for time to get things done for the church. So I got a bright idea that would save me some time. (My bright ideas are usually not so good.) I decided that I could pick up Carol for our planned time together. I would take her on a drive while I made a few stops to run some errands and gather a few things for a special program at the church. As you can imagine, that didn't go over very well. I found out that she didn't want to be a tag-along on the pursuit of my agenda. If this was to be our time, then I would have to sacrifice my to do list so that we could pursue a mutual agenda of enjoying each other and building our relationship.

If we devote time each week to express our love for God, and if our **marriage is a picture of our relationship with God, then we need to devote time each week to express our love to our spouse.** It may not always be easy but it will be worthwhile. This commitment to quality time together can be a powerful force for change.

On Christmas Day in 1998, Jimmy LaGarenne presented his wife, Nanci, with divorce papers. They were both devastated, but not surprised. Their marriage had been hurting for a while. Married at nineteen, the LaGarenne's had drifted apart over the years. Money problems and family problems ate away at their happiness. Jimmy had an affair, and Nanci began spending more time with her friends and her work. It's a story that has been repeated in a million other marriages around the country.

But on that day when Jimmy handed Nanci the divorce papers, he looked into her eyes. And suddenly, they both knew that they were making a huge mistake. So Jimmy and Nanci LaGarenne decided to save their marriage. They began going out on dates again. They kept a journal of their daily thoughts and feelings to share with one another. Jimmy began leaving Nanci love notes. Soon, the two had fallen in love again.

In October of 2000, *Redbook Magazine* sponsored a contest asking readers to send in their true love stories. The best story would win a $15,000 prize and would be turned over to a professional romance writer to be turned into a published romance novel. Jimmy sent in his story and won. *Within a Whisper* is the title of the book detailing Jimmy and Nanci LaGarenne's true love story (*Your Greatest (true) Love Story* by Joan Smith *Redbook* Oct. 2001 p. 98).

Time each week with your spouse will require three P's to be put into place. The first "P" stands for **Priority.** Commitment is never easy – it always requires sacrifice. What do you have to sacrifice in order to make sure that you devote time together? It is necessary that we value our Sabbath time with the Lord as well as with our spouse so that nothing will divert us from this priority.

The second "P" is **Plan.** Time each week with your spouse will require a plan. What is a good time that works for both of you? Agree and commit! Finding a time that works is probably the biggest obstacle. Once you have a plan, both of you will have to take responsibility for making the plan work. Husbands and wives should hold each other accountable and not become passive aggressive regarding the plan. Don't sit back and blame the other person, but take responsibility to make it happen. Rather than sitting back and waiting for your spouse to fail, you could begin reminding them the day before. This mutual sense of responsibility is what will give the greatest chance of success to your Sabbath time together.

A major objection is the potential cost of dating again. Most couples today are trying to just make ends meet and can hardly afford to add additional recreation to the budget. What I am suggesting is not costly. It could be a couple hours on the sofa, time in the backyard, taking a walk around the block or through the park, or maybe time at the table over tea. Time set aside to talk takes no money, just commitment.

The last "P" is **Preparation.** In order for you to experience time each week it will require preparation. If you fail to plan, you plan to fail. Preparing means putting away distractions and providing enhancements. Anything that will subtract from the quality of the time together should be accounted for and set aside. If the telephone is a problem then agree that you will allow voice mail to take messages. If the children are of a

Remember to save one day for the Lord.

distracting age, then maybe a babysitter would help. These distractions require preparations in order to remove them from the time together. On the other hand you can also plan for enhancements that will maximize your time. Cleaning the house, candles for a special dinner, or maybe picking up a good movie for the two of you to enjoy will require some preparation. If it is a priority, and you agree to a plan, as well as prepare for success, you will be able to spend quality Sabbath time together.

Application Questions

1. Do I spend quality time with my spouse?
2. How can we improve this part of our relationship?
3. What are the roadblocks that get in our way?
4. Have passive-aggressive tendencies gotten in the way?

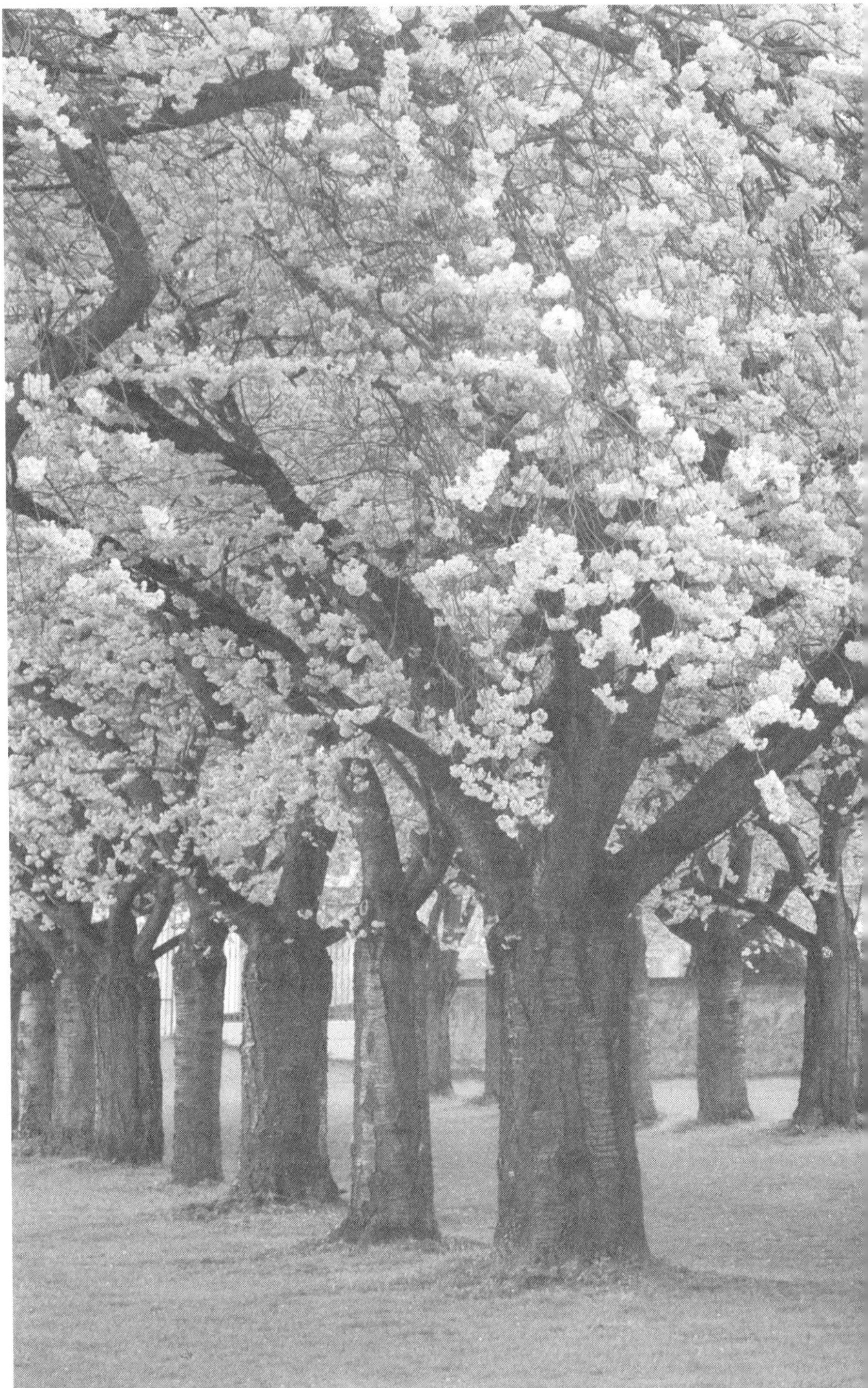

COMMANDMENT 5

"Honour your father and your mother..."

Deuteronomy 5:16

Honour your parents while cleaving to your spouse.

2 Tablets for Your Marriage

The command given to all men back in the Garden of Eden is to leave your mother and father and cleave to your wife. This for many has seemed to set up a contradiction. The fifth commandment being the first with promise of long life in the land that God was giving to the Israelites, moves us in the opposite direction to the command given in the garden. Rather than being told to leave our parents, here we are being told to honour our parents. How then do we both leave our parents and cleave to our spouse while honouring our parents? These two principles are not mutually exclusive.

We have all heard of mommy's boys who have a hard time cutting the apron strings. We all know that parents know exactly how to press those guilt buttons to urge us to do what they want. Therefore it is necessary to have some guiding principles to help us satisfy both these requirements for a successful marriage.

A parallel and instructive dilemma exists in our relationship with the government authority over us. We are told to obey the governing authorities, recognizing that God has appointed them. However, our obedience to the civil rule has a limit. We obey the government until it asks us to disobey God who represents a higher authority in our lives. In other words, we honour the government while cleaving to a higher priority in our lives. As with any human authority, **we follow that authority unless it contradicts what is required by our relationship with God.**

In much the same way, we have grown up being taught to obey our parents. This requirement to obey does not have an age restriction. You never outgrow the command to honour your mother and your father. That should be our desire until the day our parents die. However when we get married we now take on a higher priority. Our new family now becomes the greater authority in our lives. **When you got married you transferred your first responsibility and your authority from your parents to your spouse.** While parents remain a significant responsibility, marriage brings us into a new relationship and under a new authority.

If our marriage then is a picture of our relationship to Christ, then we follow other authorities, including our parents, unless

Honour your parents while cleaving to your spouse.

they ask us to do something that contradicts what is needed for a healthy relationship with our spouse. When parents place unrealistic expectations and pressures, it is critical to remember that we are to cleave to our spouse while we honour our parents.

Let me share a couple of rules to follow as we seek to honour both these priorities in our lives. First of all, when there is a problem with one of the parents, let the child of that parent deal with the problem. If I have a disagreement with my mother, it can be smoothed over very easily and we all can sit down around the Thanksgiving table in harmony. On the other hand, if my wife gets into a spat with my mother, that tension can last a long time. The saying is true that blood is thicker than water! Sometimes husbands want to jump in with in-laws and straighten them out. This can have devastating and long term effects.

There are times when the child of the parent is not equipped or strong enough to effectively deal with the problem that the parent is presenting. In these cases the second best choice is for both husband and wife to go together in agreement concerning the problem and the solution. In either case, be unified by coming to agreement about how the balance will be maintained. One of the common areas of tension surrounds the area of how you plan to spend the holidays. Every parent would love to have all the children and grandchildren around for special holidays. They can exert undue pressure to try and make it happen. In that case it is necessary to come to an agreement about how we can honour our mother and father while leaving and cleaving to our new family priority. For example alternating visits between the in-laws and including holiday time with your own family could be planned out and agreed to.

After more than 35 years of marriage I have had to learn to say no to my parents because my wife comes first. We are trained from birth to automatically do what our parents say. There are two groups that especially have to struggle with this issue. Newlyweds have to learn to make their spouse the primary responsibility while still honouring their parents. The young man must learn to cut the apron strings and make his wife the primary human relationship. This problem is not exclusively a male problem however. Young women often give deference to their mothers at the expense of the relationship with the husband. Learning to honour your parents in the context of a healthy marriage is foundational for a good marriage.

The second group which struggles with balancing the needs of parents with the needs of the spouse is the middle aged couple whose parents are now older and very needy. Caring for aging parents can complicate this balance. This issue is close to home for me as I write this book. My parents require a lot of help. I have been the power of attorney for both my mother and father and I have taken care of all of their financial concerns and made decisions on behalf of their welfare. This can be time-consuming and always needs to be balanced against the needs of my wife and family. There are a growing number of middle-aged couples struggling to honour their parents while leaving and cleaving to their spouse. Since older people are living longer and health care options are presenting more choices, it is critical that couples talk through the issues that the aging parents present.

A good starting point is for both spouses to agree that it is their desire to honour their parents. All the particulars can be worked out if both of you agree that your desire is to see what is best for both sets of parents. I want what is best for Carol's mother and Carol wants what is best for my parents. From that foundation we can hammer out the amount of time and resources to be spent on that priority without violating the responsibility to our own family.

The fulfillment of this commandment requires going back to the priority wheel that we introduced in an earlier chapter. In order to leave, cleave, and honour there must be the realization that no spoke in the wheel that God has given to us should be neglected. When we have a love for our parents as well as a love for our spouses which reflects our love for God, we are able to demonstrate the Great Commandment in our practice.

It seems like yesterday when I remember how I would rush home from middle school to fly to meetings with my father in his Cessna 172. I remember so clearly how my mom would fix

Honour your parents while cleaving to your spouse.

breakfast for us and send us off to school in the mornings. But now, in what seems like no time at all, as a father myself and serving as the pastor of Montco Bible Fellowship, I am acting as power of attorney and taking care of their business affairs. So I moved quickly from obedient child to an adult who desired to cleave to my wife as well as to honour my parents. Over several years of caring for parents, I have come to appreciate the balancing act that the Lord through this commandment requires of us. It is this tension that every married person with living parents must deal with. Complying with this commandment requires that we learn to live in this tension and leave and cleave, while honouring mother and father.

Application Questions

1. What are the challenges that our parents present to us?
2. How can we improve our attitude toward our parents, in what practical ways can I honour them?
3. What would it look like for you to leave and cleave?

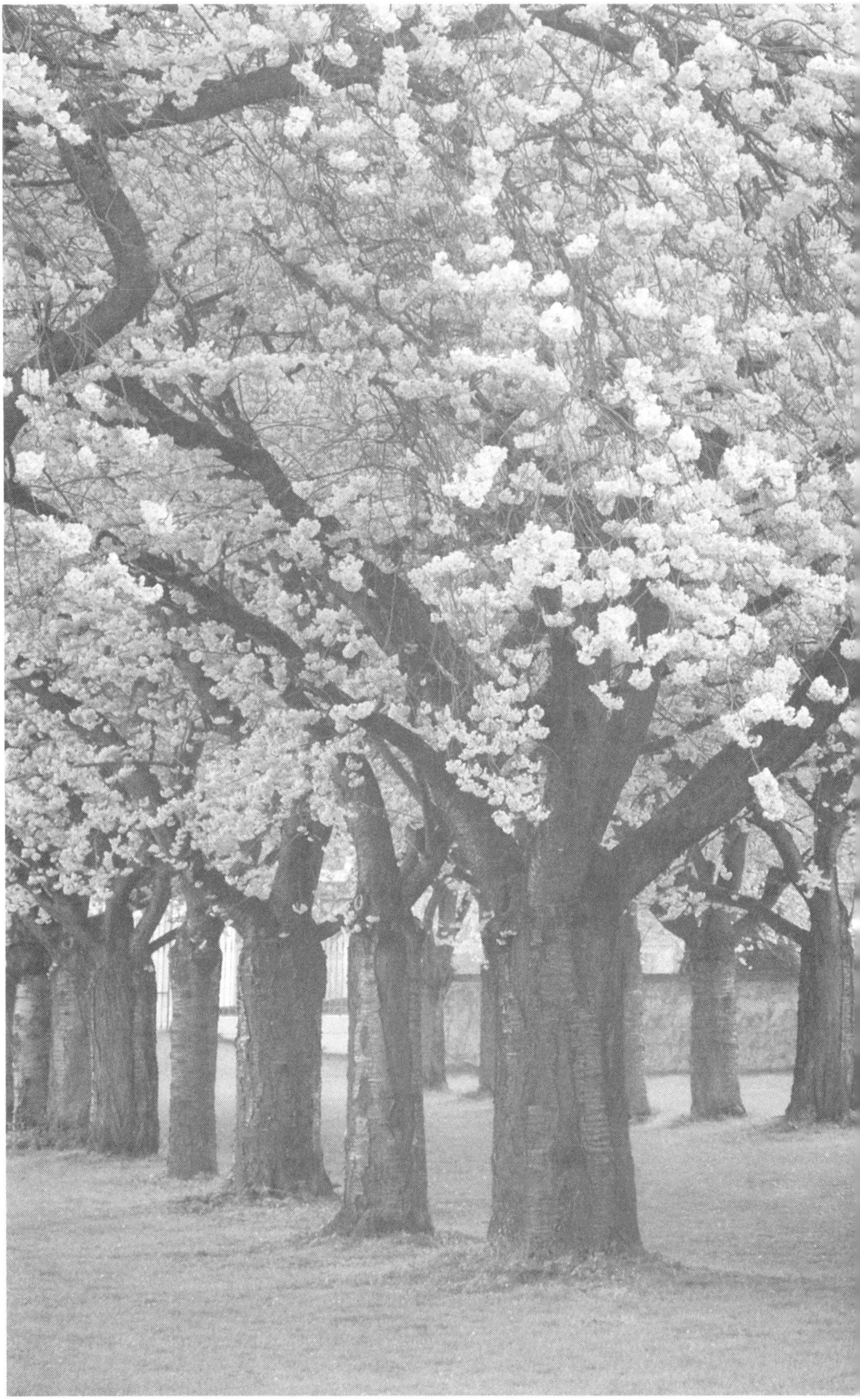

COMMANDMENT 6

"You shall not murder."

Deuteronomy 5:17

Always promote the best life for your spouse.

The opposite of murder is to promote life. It is a call to value life. Our world has little respect for a life if it does not return more than a utilitarian value to society. So we find it easy to do away with the unborn that gets in the way of our pursuits, or the aged who burden us and are unproductive. Our utilitarian valuation of life has placed ourselves at the centre of the universe. We ascribe little value to whatever and whoever does not meet our needs or serve our interest. The biblical assessment however, is clear that human life is sacred. We have been created in the image of God to be in relationship with God and to experience love for each other. The rich are not more sacred than the poor, nor are those who produce in our economy more sacred than those that society has to support.

We should value all human life and place a priority on promoting the life of our spouse. Jesus said that if you don't have love in your heart for your brother, you have committed murder (Matt. 5:22). It is helpful at this point to define love. **Love is giving my life for the welfare of someone else, without requiring anything in return.** This definition which I have borrowed and modified from different sources raises a few questions which need discussion. First of all, there have been some who have twisted this definition a little to say that love does not expect anything in return. I disagree, because we should have expectations of each other. Marriage cannot function properly without expectations. Love, however, endures even when our expectations are not met. Love does not require certain conditions to be met in order for the love to prosper. I am committed to love my wife even when my expectations are not met, and I am glad that she does not give up on me when I so often fail to meet her expectations.

The modern marriage has incorporated the idea that marriage is to be a partnership. This idea has built into it the requirement that each person carry their respective part of the burden. So the partnership can work only as long as the partnership is running properly. This contributes significantly to dissatisfaction among couples today. Whether the symptom is finances, or moral unfaithfulness, the partnership approach to marriage contributes to the conclusion that it is not working for my benefit anymore.

Always promote the best life for your spouse.

Marriage should not be a 50-50 partnership. As much as we may be tempted to see this as a wonderful ideal, it turns out to be destructive to marriage. The biggest problem with the 50-50 approach is being able to accurately judge when the 50% division has been reached. This is a problem, because we are sinful humans and, because of our sinful and selfish tendencies, we tend to exaggerate our contribution and undervalue the other person's contribution. So, as a husband, when I head out the door to go to my office in the morning, I tend to undervalue the contribution of my wife who is a homemaker and works at home. I imagine her at home and able to lie down whenever she wants. So I think, "What a life!" Meanwhile I can imagine that she pictures me at my desk with my feet up while on the phone. Her conclusion may also be, "What a life! I have all this drudgery and housework and he gets to go out and have all the fun." Both of us are devaluing the other person's contribution and effort while over valuing our own contribution.

This selfish appraisal of the partnership will result in a growing resentment and bitterness. When we see an older couple that is constantly snapping at each other, it is the result of years of thinking that they are doing more than their fair share. As the years go by bitterness grows from feeling that you have been carrying more than your fair share of the load. I spoke to a couple not long ago who expressed the resentment that was growing as each of them felt that the other was not fulfilling the requirements of an effective partnership. Unfortunately this is too often the result of entering into marriage as a partnership.

Love means that you are willing to give 100%. Love means that you are willing to make a sacrifice of your life for the welfare of the other person. I tell young couples in pre-marital counseling that they should not walk down the aisle and say "I do" unless they are willing to strap the entire relationship on their back and carry 100% on themselves. This is not only theory but we are all only one Dr.'s visit or one accident away from having to carry all the burden of the relationship ourselves.

My younger sister in Baltimore has been married now for over 25 years. She has raised three wonderful children. About a year after she was married her husband developed a tumor in his brain. It has totally disabled him and after several strokes and surgeries over the years he has spent years as a paraplegic. Since he is bound to a wheel chair and requires extra nursing help my sister has gone back into the workforce and taken up the role of bread earner, homemaker, child raiser, and all without any help from her husband.

Now consider what it would have been like if she entered into marriage with the idea that this was to be a 50-50 partnership. She would have decided that the partnership was not working and she could easily have justified leaving her husband as so many have. Any single parent who has had to carry the load all by themselves would appreciate help. Rather than bitterness over our mates not living up to our imaginary 50% requirement, we should consider with gratitude that we don't have to carry 100% all by ourselves.

The best example, other than Christ Himself, of the kind of love that gives 100% while not requiring anything in return, is a mother and her baby. Why would a mother continue to give of herself and change diapers and get awakened at all hours of the night for a baby who could not provide any help around the house? The baby can't get a job and make a contribution. The baby has nothing to offer toward the welfare of the mother. So what is in the deal for the mother?

All the mother gets out of the arrangement is to see the child develop and grow into the full potential of a well adjusted adult. The first time the baby rolls over is a thrilling moment. When the baby takes its first steps the moment is captured on video and met with much joy. When the little child goes off to school for the first time it produces such pride as to cause the parents to conclude that it was worth it all.

In the same way that love for a baby is all about the welfare of that little one, love for our spouse should be all about their welfare. Why is it that we can love our family members that way but when it comes to our spouse all of a sudden it becomes about my happiness, my fulfillment, and my feelings? To love is to be focused on the other person's welfare rather than on a selfish

Always promote the best life for your spouse.

concern for ourselves. While love is supposed to be about giving for the benefit of others, the world has successfully turned our focus inward so that this selfish focus has become the normal. Even our love songs are filled with lyrics like "you complete me", "you make me happy", "you satisfy me"…me, me, me, me, me. That is not love. That is pure selfishness. True love is focused on the other person. It is sacrificing myself so that the loved one will be complete, will be fulfilled, will be happy. That needs to be our goal and the source of our joy.

Jesus is our perfect example — *"For God so loved the world that He gave His only begotten Son, that whoever believes in Him should not perish but have everlasting life"* (John 3:16). All we have to do is accept His offer of love with the faith of a little child. That was not a benefit for God because we had nothing to offer. God gets nothing out of the deal except the joy of seeing us cleansed, sanctified, and glorified as His bride. God's agape love for us is the kind of self-sacrificing love that we are called to have for each other. If we are going to be disciples of Christ, we must be willing to follow Him in His example of love.

This commandment calls on our marriages to reflect that unconditional love which will promote the best life for our spouse. How can I demonstrate that kind of love in my marriage? What is the big enemy? Pride and selfishness are the big challenges to be overcome if we are to succeed in loving without requiring anything in return. I have said many times that the essence of our sin is selfishness. It was what Adam and Eve struggled with when they were told that there was more to be had than God was giving them. It is the symptom of sin's presence that every child, except Christ, has been born with ever since the fall.

Most Americans have a hard time with the doctrine of original sin which says that a newborn baby is a sinner. They object because the little baby has never told a lie, never killed anyone, nor said a bad word. Yet any mother will tell you that the most selfish person in the house is that little baby. The baby wants the bottle in his mouth and doesn't care what is in your mouth. One of the first jobs of the parent is to teach the little one that the world is bigger than just them. We have to teach them to share their toys and consider the feelings of others. This is true because we have all inherited a virus of sin from our parents and they from their parents, all the way back to the original couple that fell in the garden.

Execution of this commandment to promote the life of our mate is accomplished by maintaining our focus on the welfare of our spouse.

You cannot promote the best if you are not familiar with the individual needs of the person you live with. We understand by the Hebrew language used, that to "know" and be "known" is at the very heart of what marriage is all about. "To be known and still be loved is one of the supreme goals of marriage" (Sproul, p. 12).

In Genesis 2:25 we read that Adam and Eve were naked together and yet not ashamed. They were totally exposed to each other with all of their warts and wrinkles and yet with no fear of rejection. They were known and still loved.

When two sinners attempt to live together for a lifetime they need to experience that kind of acceptance while being fully aware of the strengths and weaknesses of the other. Anything less than unconditional love and understanding will cause us to fall short of this commandment to promote the best in the other person. R. C. Sproul has devised a simple test which is helpful in determining how well we know each other. Each party is to write on a piece of paper 10 things that they would like their partner to do for them. Be specific not "make me feel loved" but specify actions desired. Then on the other side write another list of ten things that your spouse would like for you to do for them. When you do this exercise it will demonstrate room for improvement in getting to know your spouse and will also provide a path toward promoting the life of the other. (Sproul, p. 28)

The irony of sacrificing yourself for the welfare of the other person and promoting their life ahead of your own is that the glory comes back to you. Just as we become trophies to God's glory as He promotes our lives, we also receive the glory as those around us flourish and we promote their lives.

Always promote the best life for your spouse.

Application Questions

1. What are the requirements that we hold as conditions for our love?
2. How can we maintain expectations without making them requirements?
3. How far am I willing to go in loving my spouse?

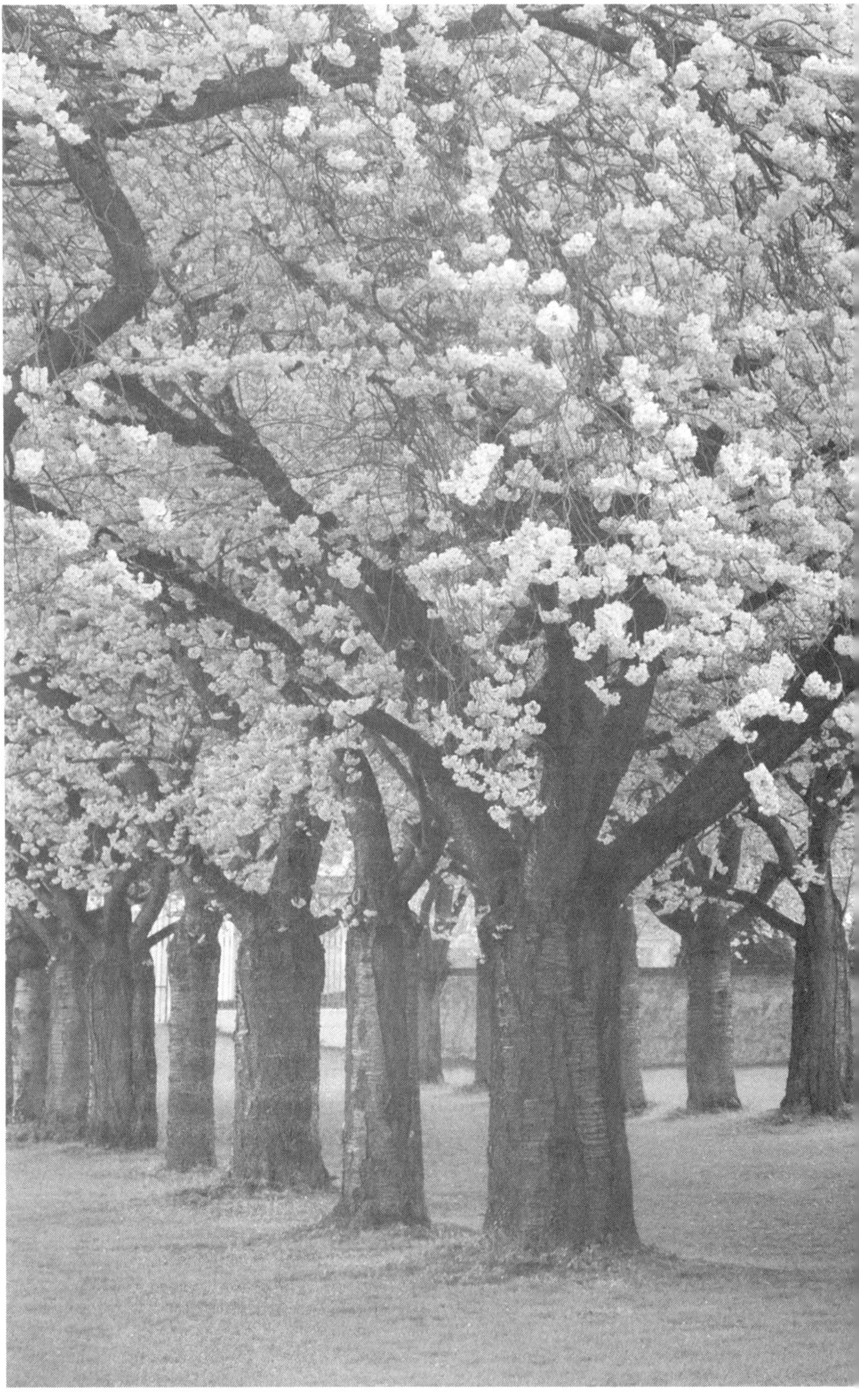

COMMANDMENT 7

"You shall not commit adultery."

Deuteronomy 5:18

Don't let anyone take the place of your spouse.

We need to start here by defining what we mean by adultery. A survey of the Old Testament reveals that when the Lord used this term he was not thinking necessarily about illicit sexual activity behind closed doors at a motel. When it comes to our relationship with God adultery is defined as **allowing anyone other than God to be God to us.** Hosea 1:2; says, *"The land has committed great harlotry by departing from the Lord"* (NKJV). God describes adultery as not seeking after the Lord and not placing Him first in your affections but rather filling that place in your heart with other people and things. In Hosea 2:2 this practice of allowing others to take the place of God in our lives is equated with a whore who seeks satisfaction from someone other than husband or wife. The Israelites were constantly turning to other gods, and so the Lord called them harlots and adulterers throughout the Old Testament.

Adultery in our marriages, as they represent our relationship with the Lord, needs to be defined in the same way. **Therefore adultery occurs anytime we look outside of the marriage relationship to meet significant personal needs whether physical or emotional.** Jesus, as he delivered the Sermon on the Mount, stated that if you even look on a woman who is not your wife you have committed adultery already in your heart (Matt. 5). That applies to both genders, not just to men. The point that Jesus was making was that the issue of adultery is not about a sexual act but rather a condition of the heart. We allow our hearts to be drawn toward other loves when our hearts should have Jesus firmly in first place and meeting our important needs.

Selfishness drives us to adultery. As we noted in an earlier chapter, selfishness moves us in the opposite direction to love. While love is giving to others, selfishness is concerned with ourselves. Whenever our first priority is to have our needs met then the feelings of others take a distant second. Our needs become our idol and our commitment to God, to our spouse, and to others become victims of our adultery.

This tendency toward adultery is demonstrated in the rise of pornography as a huge factor in our society. The increased availability of pornography with the advent of the internet,

Don't let anyone take the place of your spouse.

cable TV, and "discreet mailings" have brought this latent selfishness to the surface. It is portrayed as victimless and yet so many marriages have been strained because of the adulterous desire to have needs satisfied outside the marriage which should be satisfied only inside the marriage relationship.

What is it that drives us to look outside the marriage to meet sexual satisfaction? The factors seem to be different for men and women. Let's take the men first. Men, as the hunters, are looking for an ego stroke from someone other than their spouse. The "seven year itch" coincides with the time that men begin to wonder if they still are attractive to the opposite sex. The need to have that confirmation and to have their ego stroked is what drives men toward adultery. Some have suggested that if the wife only took good care of him at home he would not go out. While appreciation shown at home can help, the fact is that the need for that ego stroke comes from a selfish place in us and will discount the admiration of the wife. If a man finds himself needing to be noticed by others he is ripe to fall prey into an adulterous relationship. There will always be that coworker or friend at work who will be willing to stroke that ego for you and meet that need. Your commitment to God and to your spouse has to come before the needs of your ego.

Women on the other hand are usually drawn by a different motivation. Women are looking to feel appreciated, special, or cherished. When that need becomes a driving force in life she is at risk. There will always be a man that will be ready to tell her what she wants to hear. It is important that both women and men, with their differing emotional needs, should never look outside of the relationship with God and the marriage to meet those needs.

Psychologists tell us that there is an excitement and physical reaction that comes with a new relationship. This physical reaction and corresponding positive feeling is so easily misinterpreted as love. Never mistake this infatuation for love. Love is not a feeling; it is a commitment to give of yourself for the welfare of the other person without requiring anything in return. When the inevitable challenges of any relationship surface those positive feelings will dissipate and will be sustained only when they are accompanied by a commitment to sacrifice.

When a married person entertains those feelings of infatuation it is adultery! That adultery takes place in the heart long before it involves any sexual activity. It is important then for us to protect our hearts by setting our minds on the Lord and delighting ourselves in our spouses. What are you looking for and who are you expecting to provide it? Identify exactly what it is that you are looking for.

There should be some things that you recognize that only your spouse can do for you. To allow anyone else to meet those needs is adultery. If meeting that need becomes more important to you than your relationship, then that thing becomes an idol. Is it something that only God can do for you? If it is a God thing that is missing in your life, then to look to have that need met outside of your relationship with God is committing adultery against the Lord. Things like appreciation, respect, happiness, caring, can become idols that drive us outside of the relationship with God and our spouse in order to fulfill them.

I remember when my father became a private pilot in order to reach far away churches and get back home without spending nights away. I developed a real interest in flying during those years and if you had asked me what I wanted to be as a teenager I would have said a pilot without hesitation. I flew with my dad to many meetings, not because I wanted to go to church, but because I wanted to fly. It was at one of these meetings that a button on my dad's jacket fell off and a dear lady at the meeting offered to sew it back on for him. It seemed strange to me then that his answer was,"No thank you, my wife will take care of that when I get home." I understand now that there were some things that my mom did for him, and he wouldn't allow anyone else to meet those needs that she handled personally.

With the advent of online chat rooms and e-mail it has become much easier to have inappropriate private conversations with others outside of the marriage. Looking for understanding and someone to listen is often an attraction for many. Sometimes it is simply the opportunity to say things that you

Don't let anyone take the place of your spouse.

would never have the nerve to say to someone in person. No matter what encouraged the contact, the relationship can produce the same feelings of infatuation that face-to-face relationships can produce. This emotional need that is being met can become addictive and confused with love.

The fulfillment of this commandment to not commit adultery in our marriages means that we have to be very careful to not think that others can meet those needs that only our spouses should meet. Even when you feel that your needs are not being properly met by your spouse, it is sin and breaking God's moral law to step outside of the marriage bond to meet needs that should be met inside of marriage. If the first two commandments remind us to make sure that God remains in first place, this commandment reminds us that with God in first place we can also keep our spouses in a place in our lives that will satisfy the deepest needs in our hearts.

Application Questions

1. What needs do I find unfulfilled in my life?
2. Are these desires that only God can fill?
3. Are they desires that only my spouse should fill?
4. What would it look like for me to not place those desires ahead of my relationship with God and my spouse?

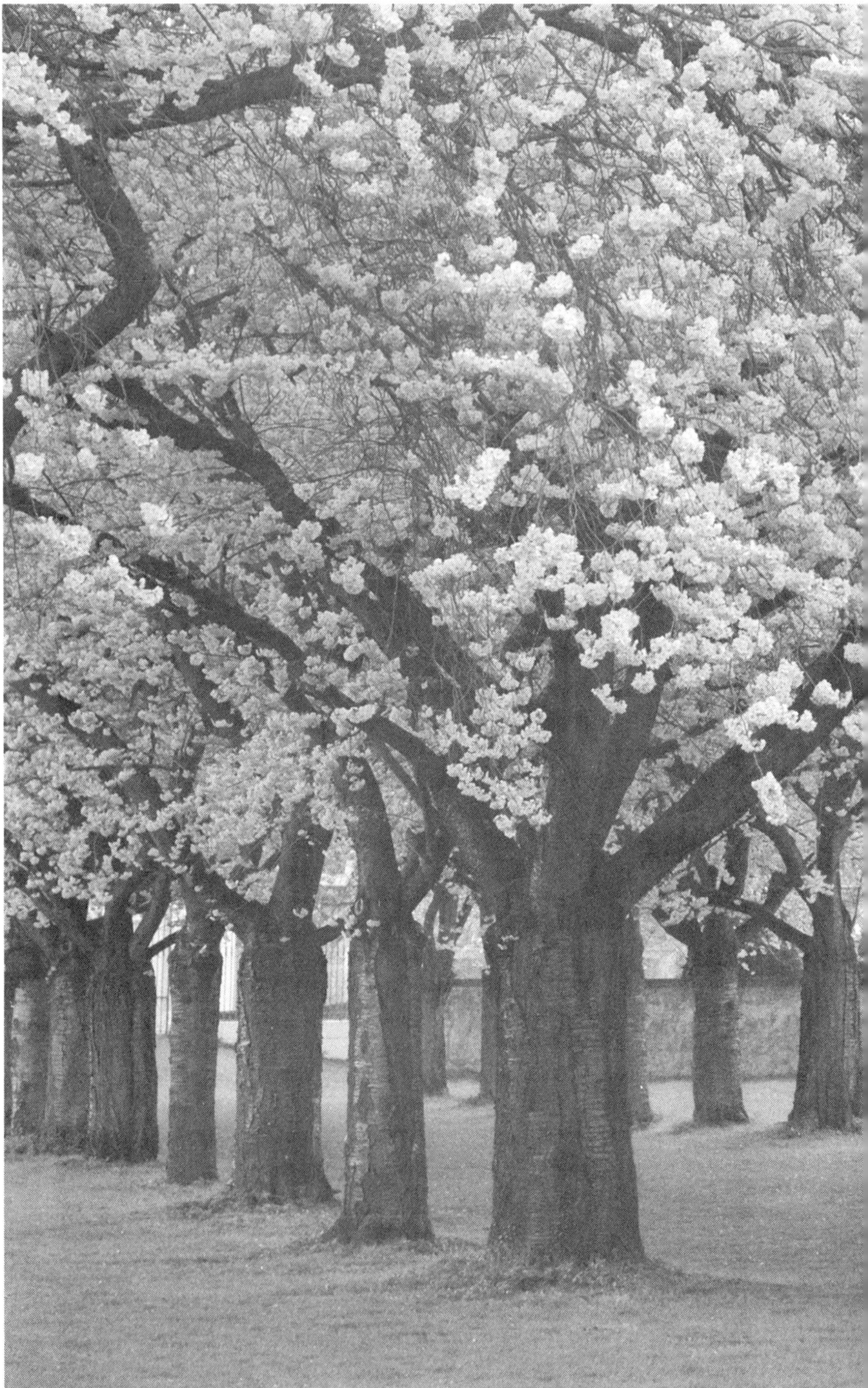

COMMANDMENT 8

"You shall not steal."

Deuteronomy 5:19

Don't take away anything that your spouse is due.

The eighth commandment tells us that we are not to steal. You may wonder what this has to do with the relationship with your spouse. There are several things that you owe your spouse and to not give what you owe is stealing. When something is promised to someone else, to keep it from them is taking what no longer belongs to you.

First of all, you owe it to your spouse to keep your vows. I think that it is a good idea to record the vows that you make on your wedding day. So often the promises that are made are all but forgotten. We certainly don't pay enough attention to make sure that we are adhering to the things that we promised. I have performed several weddings during the course of my ministry and I often wish that I had the practice of recording the vows made during the ceremonies. Those recordings would certainly come in handy during the counseling sessions that so often follow a few years of marriage.

This commandment requires that we keep our commitments and honour our word. We live in a culture where our word does not mean much. We so easily excuse ourselves from keeping promises that we have made because it is no longer convenient. From time to time our church coordinates banquets and various functions which require promising a count to a restaurant or hotel. Without fail, a percentage of those who have committed to come never show up. If 200 people say that they will be there you can safely tell the hotel 185. When you hear their excuses, the real problem becomes apparent... "I was tired", "I needed to shop for groceries", "a show was in town that I wanted to see". The issue for so many of us is that we need to value our word above our own satisfaction.

Psalm 15 asks the question, *"Who may abide in Your tabernacle? Who may dwell in Your holy hill?"* In other words, who is it that God is pleased with and approves of so that he may approach the presence of God and fellowship with Him? The Psalmist begins to list a number of the qualities of such a person. He includes in his list at the end of verse 4, *"He who swears to his own hurt and does not change."* This is a major challenge for modern day Christians who value ease and convenience even

Don't take away anything that your spouse is due.

above their word. If it will cause me pain to keep my word to you, then I may excuse myself.

We promise to love and care for each other till death. But that applies only as long as it is convenient and satisfying for me. As soon as it is causing me hurt then I will simply excuse myself. This commandment challenges us to never excuse ourselves from the commitment we have made to love till death. In other words, I owe my spouse my whole life, till death. We don't have the option to change the terms mid-stream.

You also owe your spouse your affections. That includes your body, your time, your attention, and your love. 1 Corinthians 7 talks about keeping your commitment to meet the sexual needs of your spouse. Sex then is not a reward that you give, but a commitment that you keep. It is not to become a carrot offered for good behavior or a tool used for power in the relationship. Most spouses do not see this as a commitment and a debt owed to and promised to their spouse. Sex is often withheld in the marriage due to three factors: 1. The control factor 2. The guilt factor 3. The physical factors including roughness, menopause symptoms, pregnancy, or physiological failure (Sproul, p. 94-99). These factors are to be worked on, and help from a counselor may be needed. The bottom line is that we are called to do all that we can to meet our spouse's sexual needs.

Remember that love is focused on the other person's needs and so never demands that affection be given. Love would never pressure the other person beyond expressing the need that is felt for their affection and sexual satisfaction.

To fulfill this obligation build these three habits into your relationship:

1. Say, "I love you."
2. Touch everyday in a non-sexual context.
3. Ask, "How can I show you that I love you?" and be willing to do it.

This area of paying the debt of affection to our spouse requires selfless dedication to the welfare and satisfaction of the other. Unfortunately, laziness and selfishness prevent affection from being freely expressed in our relationships. A multitude of roadblocks spring up to hinder us from accomplishing this obligation. Arguments, anger, frustration, and personal satisfaction from the relationship all take their toll on the affection being shown to our partners. The hardest thing to do is to make it not about us but to keep the focus of our hearts on pleasing God and loving our spouse.

You also owe your spouse your resources. If marriage is a picture of our relationship with Christ, then in the same way that we acknowledge that everything we have belongs to God, we have to be willing to acknowledge that we belong to our spouse. There are many parallels between our relationship with the Lord and our relationship with our spouse—our giving to the Lord represents an important one. I am often asked if I believe in tithing. My response to those who ask about tithing is that they are asking the wrong question. Christians want to know if they are supposed to calculate the tithe before taxes or after taxes. They are concerned about making sure that they don't under-give and just as importantly that they don't over-give. Malachi warns us not to rob from the Lord and so it is a valid concern to make sure that we are giving to God what we owe.

Our giving to the Lord should be an expression of our love for the Lord. The concept of tithing began before the Law of Moses and was reinforced by the law. Remember that the law was given to us as a gauge by which to measure ourselves. So if I go to church and drop two dollars in the plate, before I start to brag about my philanthropy the law reminds me that I haven't done very much. Tithing was never intended to serve as a limit of our expression of love for God. The fact is that in my love relationship with God I owe Him everything—not 10 percent but 100 percent of everything that I have. We can trust God to supply our needs when we give Him all that we have.

If I am giving God only 10 percent then the rest belongs to me and I can go on a shopping spree to the mall. But if I give God everything then I become a steward or manager of God's money. He can tell me how much to put in the plate at church, and how much to send to that mission organization that needs

Don't take away anything that your spouse is due.

support. Before I run to the dealer and sign sixty months of His money away, I need to talk to Him about the purchase and get His approval.

I don't know how it works in your house, but at my house I receive a check each month from the church and I give it all to my wife. Not ten percent but 100 percent. How is it that a man can give his wife his paycheck? It is only because he can trust her to understand and to supply his needs. Carol understands that I need gas in the car, that I need lunch money, and that every now and then I need a new pair of shoes. And so I can turn over my resources to her and trust her to meet my needs.

Our marriages are to reflect our relationship with God, and we are not to rob from our spouses. In the same way that we are to give 100 percent to God, we owe our spouses 100 percent of all that we have.

I have spoken to many young ladies, especially from the Caribbean islands who have been advised by their mothers to tuck away a little account for themselves and not to let their husbands know about it. The principle that I would like to leave with you from this commandment is that since the goal of marriage is oneness, to the extent that there is his money and her money there is not oneness. I am not telling anybody what they can or cannot do, only that if there is his money and her money there is not oneness. That does not mean that there can't be two accounts or that she can't operate out of an account that he leaves alone. Oneness however requires that it is all our money and the accounts can still be joint accounts.

There are circumstances where this ideal is not possible and not wise. For example if a spouse proves to be untrustworthy due to an addiction to drugs or gambling. Maybe there is constant budget busting and over-spending which jeopardizes the family finances. In these cases it is wise to separate the funds. However we must understand that this is not the ideal oneness that God would like to see in our marriages.

While love is giving of yourself without requiring anything in return, the fact is usually you get back so much in return. Robert Schuller, president of a spiritual retreat centre, and his son, both well-known pastors and authors, rave about the elder Schuller's mother's ministry of baking pies. Grandma Schuller's apple pies were works of culinary art, according to her family, and she often gave them away to neighbours and friends as a way to cheer people up or to let them know she cared. One woman who received this gift from Grandma Schuller was a schoolteacher who had fallen ill. Grandma brought her an apple pie to comfort her during her convalescence.

Twenty years later, Robert Schuller received a letter on his "Hour of Power" television show. A woman who had seen his show wanted to know if his mother was a woman named Jenny Schuller who baked delicious apple pies. Schuller wrote back to the woman and replied that his mother was that same Jenny Schuller. The letter writer was the schoolteacher who had received that pie so long ago. This woman left her whole life savings of $60,000 to Dr. Schuller's ministry—out of gratitude for an apple pie.

Sometimes we don't give what we owe because we don't want to be taken advantage of. Remember that God is no man's debtor and he will repay. Our ultimate trust is in God and not in man. It is out of a heart filled with love for God that we can give to Him our all and obey Him when he tells us to give of ourselves to others.

So we owe it to our spouses to love God and not to hold back from Him. Our first love is to God and so we must make sure that we don't rob God (Mal. 3:8-11). We learned from the first commandment that we owe God to love Him with all our heart. We find through the history of mankind that we have universally robbed God of the love that He is due. If we can rob God then we can more easily rob each other. In addition, when we rob God of the place in our hearts that He deserves, we also, by that negligence, rob our spouses as well.

Therefore you owe it to your spouse to not be the one to mess up the triangle. It is worth repeating that the goal of marriage is the oneness that God intended in Genesis 2:24. As the triangle illustrates, when God is at the top and both spouses are moving toward a closer relationship with God in first place in

Don't take away anything that your spouse is due.

their hearts, the result is oneness as they meet at the top of the triangle. Anytime one spouse fails to love God and chases idols he robs his spouse of the opportunity to experience the oneness at the top of the triangle. It is one thing if neither partner is pursuing God, but it is tragic when one desires to have God in first place and to live at the top of the triangle. That desire for oneness with the other in a mutual relationship with God is never realized. This is robbing the other person of the most precious experience that marriage can offer. So the commandment not to steal becomes a commandment that reinforces our need to obey the first and greatest commandment.

Lastly, you owe submission to your spouse. There has been much said about mutual submission in marriage, but usually the concept so waters down the headship of the man that it means very little. Let me try and bring a little clarity to the idea of mutual submission that is taught in Scripture. In Ephesians 5 and in Colossians 3 we find the exhortation to wives to submit to their husbands. It is necessary to say that this is not a statement about the relationship between men and women. It says nothing about the roles of women in society or in corporate America. It also says nothing about the role of women in the church. There are other verses which can inform us about that. Women are not being told to submit to men, but only to their own husbands.

This submission does not mean that wives should not voice their point of view. Men need to hear the perspective that wives bring. Their intuition, emotion, and female sense are invaluable to men. Women do a disservice by not voicing their opinion even strenuously when needed. Submission however means that after you have done all you can to inform and convince, you recognize that God will hold that man responsible as the head as you submit to his decision.

The very next verse tells the husband to love his wife. I gave a good definition of love earlier which we need to consider again here. Love is the total giving of yourself for the welfare of the other person without requiring anything in return. In other words, a husband is called to submit to the welfare of his wife. He submits his will to do only what will promote the best life for his wife. A loving husband doesn't buy for himself while his family stands in need. He doesn't spend the money that the family needs. He disciplines his will in submission to the welfare of his wife.

Mutual submission then requires the wife to submit to the will of the husband as is fitting in the Lord. And it requires the husband to submit his will to the welfare of the wife as Christ did for the church. Mutual submission does not water down the responsibility and headship of the husband as the responsible party before God in the home. It is stealing to not give our spouse the appropriate submission that God requires.

Application Questions

1. What is it that I am holding back from God and my spouse?
2. Am I robbing my spouse of the ability to experience oneness at the top of the triangle?
3. Am I giving the affection due my spouse?
4. Is there oneness in our finances?
5. In what areas is my biblical submission being withheld?

COMMANDMENT 9

"You shall not bear false witness..."
                                        Deuteronomy 5:20

Never lie to each other.

The old science question asks, "If a tree falls in the woods does it make a sound?" The answer of course depends on your definition of sound. There are frequency waves which are developed when the tree fell but those frequencies may not be considered "sound" until they are received by the ear and transmitted to the brain so that the result of the waves can be heard. Therefore under this definition sound requires both a source and a receiver.

Honest communication also requires a two way partnership between the speaker and the listener. I often ask the question, "Whose responsibility is it to arrive at understanding?" Is it the speaker's responsibility to be understood? Is it the listener's responsibility to understand? The answer is that it is a partnership and therefore both listener and speaker bear the responsibility for understanding.

It is similar to the concept of teaching. The definition of the word "teach" is to impart a skill or knowledge. Therefore simply to lecture, with no knowledge being imparted or conveyed to another person, falls short of teaching. It requires communication, which involves a partnership between the teacher and the student, just as communication requires a partnership between the speaker and the listener.

Active listening is a skill which is intended to maximize the potential of the communication. It represents a body of activity which recognizes the responsibility of both parties to arrive at accurate communication.

The communication problems which exist between husbands and wives have their roots all the way back to the sin of Adam and Eve in the garden. God discovered their transgression and called Adam in for a face-to-face in His Presence. I can imagine Eve waiting patiently and anxiously for God's decision as to their fate. As the anxiety built by the minute, Adam finally emerged from the meeting and I imagine Eve running over asking, "What did He say? What did He say?" and Adam, a typical man, no doubt shrugged and said, "Oh, nothing!" Communication in marriages has been going downhill ever since (Sproul, p. 11).

Never lie to each other.

I have come to realize that for most men, listening represents the "work of marriage". You have heard it said that marriage is hard work; well this is the hard work for most men. Undoubtedly this is a stereotype and may not be true for you as an individual. Women tend to be more verbal than men. It takes focus, effort, and sacrifice for many of us men to do well with this skill. It becomes hard when the game is tied with one minute to go, and your wife wants to talk. It is hard work when you come home and all you want to do is crash but she wants to share her day. It becomes hard work for me when I tend to daydream and my mind strays to a hundred other concerns. It is in the course of those real life situations that we must consciously focus on our wives and do the hard work of marriage. You cannot promote the best life for your spouse if you do not listen carefully and intently.

When you go to a drive thru fast food restaurant they listen to your request at the first stop you make as you shout into the menu box. But before you leave, they usually repeat your order to validate it without criticizing, correcting, or passing judgment. The corporate world has learned that, in order to avoid misunderstandings and mistakes in fulfilling requests, it is helpful to take time to make sure that accurate communication has taken place before moving forward with the information. If this is true when ordering a hamburger and fries then it certainly is true when we are trying to convey our feelings to each other. Repeating what you hear demonstrates that you understand what they are saying. Psychologists call it "active listening". You can't promote the best in the other person until you have heard and understood them.

In daily life misunderstandings are prevalent. I remember in the days before cell phones, when Carol would call and ask me to stop and pick up some groceries on the way home from the office. So without asking any questions, I would run with confidence thinking that I understood. After all, how hard could it be to get some flour from the market! Then when I arrived at the aisle where the flour is stocked I realized that they had 20 different types of flour. I would inevitably make the wrong choice and go home to a disappointed wife who would have to send me back to the store with more clarification. If I had only asked a few questions, rather than assuming I understood, that extra trip could have been avoided.

The problem is compounded when we are sharing feelings, and not simply talking about a shopping list. It is a two-fold dilemma. First of all, most of us are not professional wordsmiths, nor expert communicators. Therefore often the first thing we say and the first words we choose may not always accurately convey the feelings that we are trying to express. As a listener seeking understanding it is dangerous to run with those first expressions feeling confident that we understand. A simple question like, "So you feel sad?" may elicit clarification like, "I'm not really sad but I have been feeling lethargic". So questions offer an opportunity for the speaker to give clarification and produce greater understanding.

The second dilemma is created by the fact that we don't always understand what the other person means because so much of our communication is nonverbal and we often miss so many clues. Therefore it is dangerous to run to the bank with what we have heard and assume that understanding has been reached. Questions are an essential part of ensuring understanding and our laziness is what hinders that extra step.

One last point on active listening is that since communication is a two-way street understanding is the responsibility of both parties,—both the speaker and the listener are partners in this process and both must assume responsibility for understanding. That means that if the listener does not ask questions or fails to repeat giving an indication that there is understanding, then the speaker who desires to be understood should ask questions in order to make sure that communication has taken place. This is a place where the one speaking can fall into the trap of becoming passive aggressive by waiting for the spouse to fail, creating yet again another opportunity to blow up in anger and to criticize for a lack of understanding. The communicator must also assume the responsibility for ensuring that accurate communication has taken place. If it is our desire to experience oneness in our marriages, then bear one another's burdens and so fulfill the Law of Christ (Gal. 6:2).

Never lie to each other.

In John 17 Jesus expressed the desire that we would experience oneness in the same way that oneness is enjoyed in the Trinity. Notice that in the Trinity there is the standard of oneness which Jesus prayed would be evidenced in the disciples. Each of the Persons of the Godhead are on the same page in complete transparency. There are no hidden agendas, no secret accounts, no lies or dishonesty. This oneness in heaven becomes the goal that should be sought after here on earth in our marriages.

In Genesis 2:24 we read that God also desires for that same oneness to be expressed in the marriage relationships. Accurate and honest communication becomes a necessary ingredient in order to accomplish this goal. There are many things that can wear away at the oneness. Money, priorities, culture, communication skills, in-laws, secrets, unshared feelings, pride, are all hindrances which prohibit the oneness that we seek. The greatest need in marriage however is the need for honesty. **The greatest barrier to oneness in marriage is dishonesty.**

Every lie creates another barrier to the oneness. As Carol reminds me, it is not just telling an untruth, a lie is also creating a false impression by leaving out the whole truth. Oneness can be experienced only in the context of an open, vulnerable, relationship. Excuses such as "I don't want to hurt my spouse, or it will only result in an argument", are not valid. There are Christian counselors who advise people not to rock the boat with unfaithfulness from the past or issues which may cause pain. The fact is that to the extent there are issues not yet dealt with and worked through, then to that extent you will never experience oneness.

There is some honesty that may have to be expressed in the presence of a counselor or a respected third party. Without doubt there is pain and disappointment associated with revealing yourself honestly. There may be trust issues which will have to be reestablished, but at the end of the day, what you will have is an honest relationship based on truth. With secrets, all you have is a façade and not a true relationship.

Ephesians 4:25 ties speaking the truth with unity. As members of one body we are obligated to maintain that unity with truth. Nothing will tear a relationship apart like dishonest communication. Therefore the commandment is to not bear false witness. Never tell a lie.

Pride is the big enemy to honesty. Children lie out of fear while the number one reason that adults lie is pride. The strange thing is that, while we work so hard to keep up a façade with our spouse, that is the one person who really knows us for who we are. If there is anyone in the world with whom we can take off the mask we hide behind, it is our spouse who knows us better than anyone else. We wear the mask with its frozen smile and pat answers to church, on the job, with our neighbours, but when we come home we should be able to take off the façade, lay aside the false pride and be vulnerably open and honest.

We can help our spouses by being a safe place for honesty. If we expect honesty from our spouse, then we must make sure that we are a safe place. Unfortunately, spouses have not always been that safe place where honesty can flourish. There was an incident in a church where inappropriate behaviour took place between one of the pastors and a woman in the church. The issue was brought to the attention of the elders and was being dealt with between the parties involved. The pastor told his wife about the whole matter and the wife had a trusted girlfriend with whom she shared the situation. This trusted girlfriend had a trusted girlfriend who had a trusted friend and soon it was all over the church. By this time the version of events was expanding like a fish story and what originally could have been dealt with privately according to Matthew 18 now required the involvement of the whole church. The result was that this pastor decided to step down from ministry and left the church. I am not defending him in any way. I am only sharing this story to demonstrate that as spouses we have to be very careful with the information that honest communication brings to us. We must be a safe place for honesty if we expect honesty. There should be a desire to protect the reputation of our spouse at all costs. There can be no trusted girlfriend or buddy, no prayer partner, no sounding board, that causes us to put at risk the reputation of someone that we love.

We are told that love covers a multitude of sins. (Prov. 10:12; 1 Pet. 4:8) The idea is not that love ignores sin or doesn't deal

Never lie to each other.

with it effectively. The Hebrew version of this verse has the idea that love doesn't broadcast sin. Love will not take someone's faults beyond what is needful for repentance and restitution. Love never gossips, never slanders, but will always seek to protect the person's reputation. True love is a safe place for honesty. It handles the sin of others with humility remembering the grace of God extended to them. So the question is, "Have I been a safe place?" If I am unwilling to be a safe place for my spouse to confess, then I do not deserve the honesty that I desire.

Christ is the perfect example of a safe place. He took our sin and bore it in His own body on the cross. When He could have been our worst accuser He cried out, *"Father forgive them for they know not what they do."* The hymn writer put it so beautifully, "What a friend we have in Jesus/all our sins and griefs to bear/what a privilege to carry everything to God in prayer." (*What a Friend We Have in Jesus*, Joseph Scriven). With Jesus as our model, we should seek to be a safe place for others and especially for our spouse.

If we fail to be a safe place, we contribute to the problem by adding fear to the problem of pride. **Fear plus pride is a deadly combination.** God does not give us *"the spirit of fear, but of power and of love and of a sound mind"* (2 Tim. 1:7). Unfortunately too many of us are not walking in the Spirit but rather we are walking in fear. When that fear is mixed with the pride of life, honesty is next to impossible. I am not laying the burden of your spouse's honesty at your door. Each of us has to stand before God one day. All I am suggesting is that, out of a heart of love for our mates we should be the kind of people that make it as easy as possible for others to come to and share honestly with.

Application Questions

1. How well do you actively listen in your relationship?
2. Is pride contributing to dishonesty in your relationship?
3. Am I a safe place for honesty to flourish?
4. Do I feel safe to be vulnerable with my spouse?

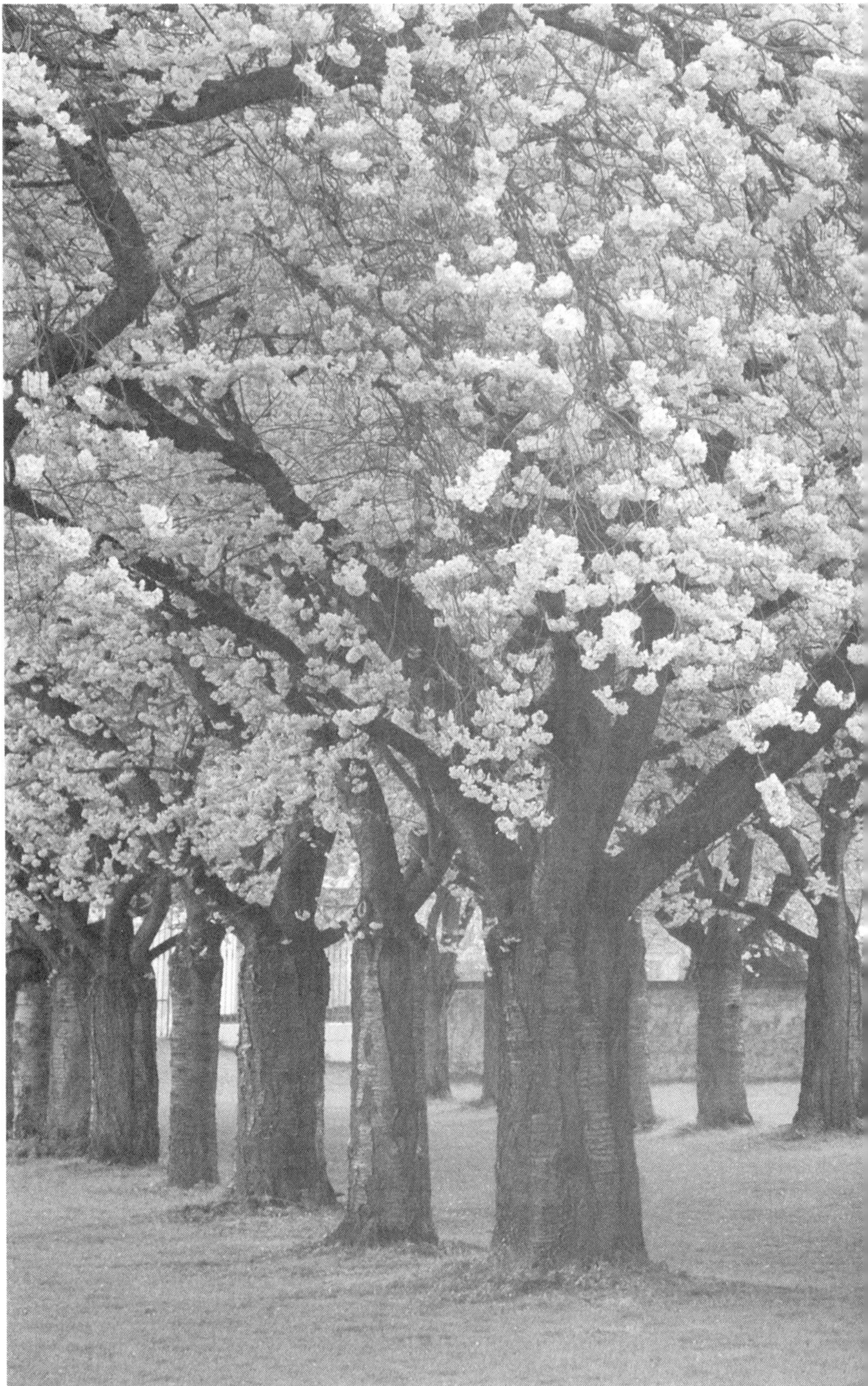

COMMANDMENT 10

"You shall not covet…"

Deuteronomy 5:21

Be content with the spouse that God has given you.

Appreciate your wife and don't be like the husband who was talking to his friend and said, "Bob, you're having an anniversary soon, right?"

Bob replied, "Yup, a big one—20 years of marriage."

"Wow," said the first man, "what are you going to get your wife for your anniversary? It's got to be something pretty special."

Bob replied, "Going on a trip to Australia."

"Wow, Australia, that's some gift!" said the first man. "That's going to be hard to beat. What are you going to do for your 25th anniversary?"

"I'll have the money to bring her back by then."

To be content means to appreciate your spouse and not to try to send her away. It means to value and not to desire to replace that gift from God for the shiny model that lives next door. The grass is always greener on the other side of the fence until you jump the fence and find out that it is just as messed up as your lawn. Many a person has jumped the fence only to realize that his own lawn looked pretty good after all.

Contentment comes from accepting the gift of your spouse as from the hands of a loving God who is working on your life conforming you into the image of Christ while at the same time changing your spouse. Difficulties in our relationships serve to make us stronger. Someone once said that if it doesn't kill you then it will make you stronger. I don't believe that God desires for us to stay in a dangerous relationship that takes us to the brink of physical harm. I do believe however that God works sanctification and change in our lives by placing us with someone who will chisel off the rough edges. That is often a painful process, but, as we exercise trust in God as He works in us through our spouse, we begin to appreciate the tools and the people that He uses to conform us into the people that He has called us to be.

What do you do then when you don't find satisfaction in your spouse? No doubt the majority of couples struggle being satisfied with the spouse that God has given them. The divorce rate alone bears that out. You may feel that your marriage was

Be content with the spouse that God has given you.

a mistake. Maybe you entered into an unwise relationship. You could be married to an unbeliever and wishing for a Christian mate. Whatever the circumstances were that got you into your marriage you can be encouraged to know that God is sovereign and when you place your current life into His hands He will renew your mind and allow you to experience that good and acceptable will of God for your life. As you trust God in your situation you will begin to appreciate those He is using around you and find contentment in God's sovereignty.

The answer then to finding satisfaction is to trust God and be content in Him! 1 Timothy 6:6 says, *"Godliness with contentment is great gain"*. Godliness is more than a list of do's and don'ts. It is walking by faith and being filled with the Spirit of God. Paul told the Colossians that the same way you received Christ by faith is how you are to walk through life. Learning to trust God through all the issues of life leads us to contentment. Through good times and bad times, in sickness and in health, for richer or poorer, God is still on the throne. When you combine walking by faith in the power of the Spirit with the contentment which is produced in our hearts, there is much gain—not necessarily monetary gain but there is the gain of the joy of the Lord. There is the gain of positive change in our lives. There is the gain of a closer relationship with God and your spouse. We are enabled to gain unity at the top of the triangle with God.

The problem is that we want more. And we look for more. The spiritual benefits seem so far away and elusive. It is so much easier to set my sights on the issues here on earth rather than on the spiritual realities. Can I be satisfied with what God has for me? The answer to that question is directly related to my ability to set my affections on things above as we are exhorted to do in Colossians 3:2. It is only as we desire the spiritual benefits that God has for us and value them more than our own lives that we will truly become content. Too many of us are willing to exchange those spiritual treasures for the physical and momentary benefits on earth.

We can be satisfied with the life we have only when we are first satisfied with the Giver of life. It is as I desire more than anything else to please God, and I value His opinion of me more than the world's opinion of me, that I can be content in His direction over my life. It is when the goal of my life is to have the Lord say *"Well done, my good and faithful servant,"* then I can find contentment in any circumstance.

Mark 8:34 tells us that to be a disciple you have to deny yourself and take up your cross daily, and, I will add, "with contentment". It is impossible to follow Jesus as a disciple as long as you value your own desires more than the spiritual blessings that He has for you. In Romans 12:1-2 we find that God's will is good, acceptable, and perfect. In other words, God has placed each of us inside a fence of His will for our lives. Inside that fence is an abundant life that we will find to be good and acceptable. The irony of this Gospel is that we will never find the abundant life until we deny our idea of what we want the abundant life to be. We must forsake all of our plans and dreams and be willing to follow Jesus into His plan for our lives.

When we fail to trust God's promise to lead us into that promised land of fulfillment, we begin to drool over the neighbour's fence. Let's resolve to trust God and present to Him our lives and our marriages, with all of the problems and shortcomings that come with it. Then we can begin to watch the Potter go to work and make something beautiful out of our marriages.

Another factor which wars against contentment in our marriages is the fact that opposites attract. Many of us have married someone who is so different than we are. Those differences become points of frustration and even aggravation. But God uses those very points of frustration to work in our lives. They are also points of balance as our strengths and weaknesses are complemented by our spouse. **Eve was different and so complemented Adam.** It helps to make a list of the ways that your spouse complements you. Look at the list and note what you appreciate and what frustrates you. Can you see how God can use the things that frustrate you in order to form you into the person that He wants you to be?

God is sovereign and knows exactly what you need. In Genesis God gave Adam a help *"meet," "suitable"*, or *"fit"* for him.

Be content with the spouse that God has given you.

He does the same thing for us today. You may not have picked the perfect spouse but be assured that before the foundation of the world God knew who you would be with today. If you will trust Him He will work it out for your good and use that person to complement your points of weakness. His sovereign rule over your life does not end even if you find yourself married to an unbeliever. While that may not have been His perfect will for you He can take you right where you are if you will surrender your desires to Him. God's uses even the unsaved to complement us and to form the image of His Son in us. I think we make a mistake when we conclude that an unsaved spouse has nothing to contribute to our spiritual growth. God is still King and is still in control of our lives. Romans 8:28 tells us that He will not allow anything to come to us but that which will work together for our good because we are called according to His purpose.

So often we don't appreciate what we need most. Speaking from my own experience, I am an optimistic and entrepreneurial person. Carol on the other hand is more inclined to see the potential problems and issues that may have to be faced. It is easy for me to see her hesitancy as a negative trait and to become frustrated by what I see as pessimism. Over the years however I have come to see that my optimism and her skepticism have made us a better team. God has a way of putting us together in ways that produce the best outcome if we will appreciate His wisdom.

How I treat the gift is a reflection of my love for the giver of the gift. As I appreciate the gift that God has given me in my spouse and trust His wisdom and sovereignty as it works itself out in my life, I will increasingly cherish the gift. I see my spouse as a gift from God and as an expression of His love and concern for me. As this becomes a reality in my thinking, when I have a problem with the gift I need to take it up with the gift-Giver. His throne of grace has a complaint department with excellent customer service. You would never sit at home and complain about a defective product that you received as a birthday gift. You would take it back to the manufacturer and ask that it be fixed. In the same way we need to learn to take the issues that we have with our spouse back to God and trust Him to work out all the defects.

It is only as we walk in that trust that we can be content even with all the defects that we perceive. I am not saying that there is never a time to leave or that you should be content with dangerous or abusive conditions. But as we trust God, He will give us wisdom and direction as to what we should do.

The big enemy of contentment is selfishness. I said earlier that the essence of the sin principle is selfishness. It is the violation of every one of the Ten Commandments. It is the reason that we struggle with each one of these commandments and especially with this last one. Since our selfish hearts always want more and are never satisfied with what we have, we are constantly looking over at our neighbour's yard and admiring the greener grass.

The fact is that the grass which looks so green from a distance turns out to be just as dry and lumpy when you spend some time in their yard. What is it that feeds our selfishness and always desires more than we have? Part of the answer I believe is that we tend to feel that we deserve more than we have. This sense of entitlement causes us to consider ourselves to have been cheated if we are getting by with less than the Jones family next door. We ask ourselves, "Why can't my family be like that family?" "Why can't my wife be like that wife?"

The opposite of this discontent comes from a heart of gratitude. A little bit of humility will remind us that God has blessed us with so much more than we deserve. If we would stop and count our blessings, naming them one by one, it would surprise us what God has done. Let's stop focusing on what we don't have. Let's stop wishing that we were like someone else or in their shoes. Let's begin to be content with the gift that God has given and trust Him to fix what needs fixing and to use the rough edges to make and mold us into the image of His dear Son.

Contentment is at the heart of the matter of submission. We are called to submit to the gift of the person that we have promised to love, submit to the working of death and deterioration in our bodies, the will and welfare of our spouse, the oneness of the two persons, the suffering of the process of sanctification and the accountability in marriage, submission to the disciplines of the Christian life. Back in 1953 this submission was

Be content with the spouse that God has given you.

identified as a disciplined suicide (Mason, p. 138). From a more positive perspective submission should be viewed as prioritizing the other person's welfare, and will. Husbands and wives are called to submit to one another as each prioritizes the welfare and will of the other over and above their own desires. It is this priority of the other which opens the door to contentment and allows us to avoid covetousness.

It is helpful here to distinguish between covetousness and jealousy. Coveting is wanting what we don't have because someone else has it. Jealousy, on the other hand, while often used as a synonym, actually refers to a fear of losing what we have to a rival. A husband may be jealous of his wife out of a fear of losing her to a more desirable man. God is a jealous God because He desires not to lose our love to the world or to self. A certain amount of jealousy over the person that we love may be normal and healthy as long as it is not paralyzing and based on mistrust. Coveting what our neighbour has is never justified. We may have goals to acquire more than we have today, but it should never be about what someone else has. After we have acquired more than we need, our drive for more usually gets fueled by materialism driven by comparison to others.

The answer then is to love God more than self. This commandment takes us right back to the first commandment. It is no accident that this commandment against coveting comes last. It calls us to loop right back to the first and greatest commandment. It is only as we love God and our neighbour more than we love ourselves that we will be able to experience victory over covetousness.

The second part of that Great Commandment is to love your neighbour as yourself. When Jesus was asked, *"Who is my neighbour?"* He told the parable of the Good Samaritan. That story simply made the point that even those we don't get along with, those who are considered outcasts, those we would even consider to be enemies are our neighbours. If that is true, then certainly the spouse we have is to be accorded the same treatment as a neighbour. Regardless of the shortcomings and issues that may be present we are to sacrifice for their wellbeing as we would for our own selves. The tendency to pull back and look out for ourselves only propels the heart toward covetousness.

There are three forces which fuel our covetousness according to 1 John 2:12-17. The lust of the flesh is the first and strongest lust which drives us to covet beyond what God has intended for us. These natural desires are intended by God to be fulfilled within specific contexts. Food, for example, is a natural desire which should be satisfied within the context of good health and concern for others. It has driven many a person however to a life of obesity and bad health due to the lack of discipline over their lust for food. The same thing can be said of the lust for sexual satisfaction. It is a God-given drive to be enjoyed in the context of a marriage. This design by God protects the family unit as well as our physical health. When we willingly ignore God's design and His rules and pursue fulfillment of these drives regardless of what God has to say then we bring destruction to families and health consequences to society. Covetousness, fueled by the lust of the flesh, can be resisted by being content to exercise the drives of the flesh within the plan of God for our lives.

The lust of the eyes refers to the desires aroused in us to possess the things that we see. All of us fight the natural desire to have the things that are flashed before us in TV commercials, magazines, and on the radio. The advertising agencies on Madison Avenue and around the country have become expert in the art of exploiting this natural desire to have what we don't have and to experience what the lust of our eyes is craving. It is a good thing that we can't afford to satisfy every urge, but too often we put ourselves in financial trouble by following the desire of our eyes beyond the financial principles that God has laid out for us to follow.

The pride of life speaks to that desire to be seen as above others. It is normal to want to be seen as significant. We all want to lead the pack and to be at the head table. God has a plan for our lives and He has given us a set of gifts which will be recognized by others as we develop those gifts. Rather than being content with the gifts and abilities, responsibility and place of ministry that God has for us, we desire more. Pride drives us to

Be content with the spouse that God has given you.

compare ourselves with others. And so choir members want to sing the solos. Pastors want to move to a bigger church. Sunday School teachers want to be the superintendent. Wives want the guy with more money. Husbands want the prettier and smarter girl. Meanwhile these lusts have caused us to sin by not being content with God's plan for our lives.

In so many ways the Great Commandment becomes the key to a happy marriage as it is the key to fulfilling the Ten Commandments. Jesus summarized the law in Matthew 22 with the Great Commandment. He makes us understand that living a life that is pleasing to God in our marriages comes down to the heart.

Jeremiah 31:3 tells us that the New Testament is all about the law being written on our hearts. In other words, God is the only one who can do the heart surgery necessary for us to be successful in applying His law in our marriages.

Application Questions

1. How does God work through my spouse for my sanctification?
2. What are the characteristics that I struggle with the most in my spouse?
3. How is it that those things can be used by God to change me?
4. Do I have a sense of entitlement for more than God has provided?
5. What is it that fuels my covetousness?

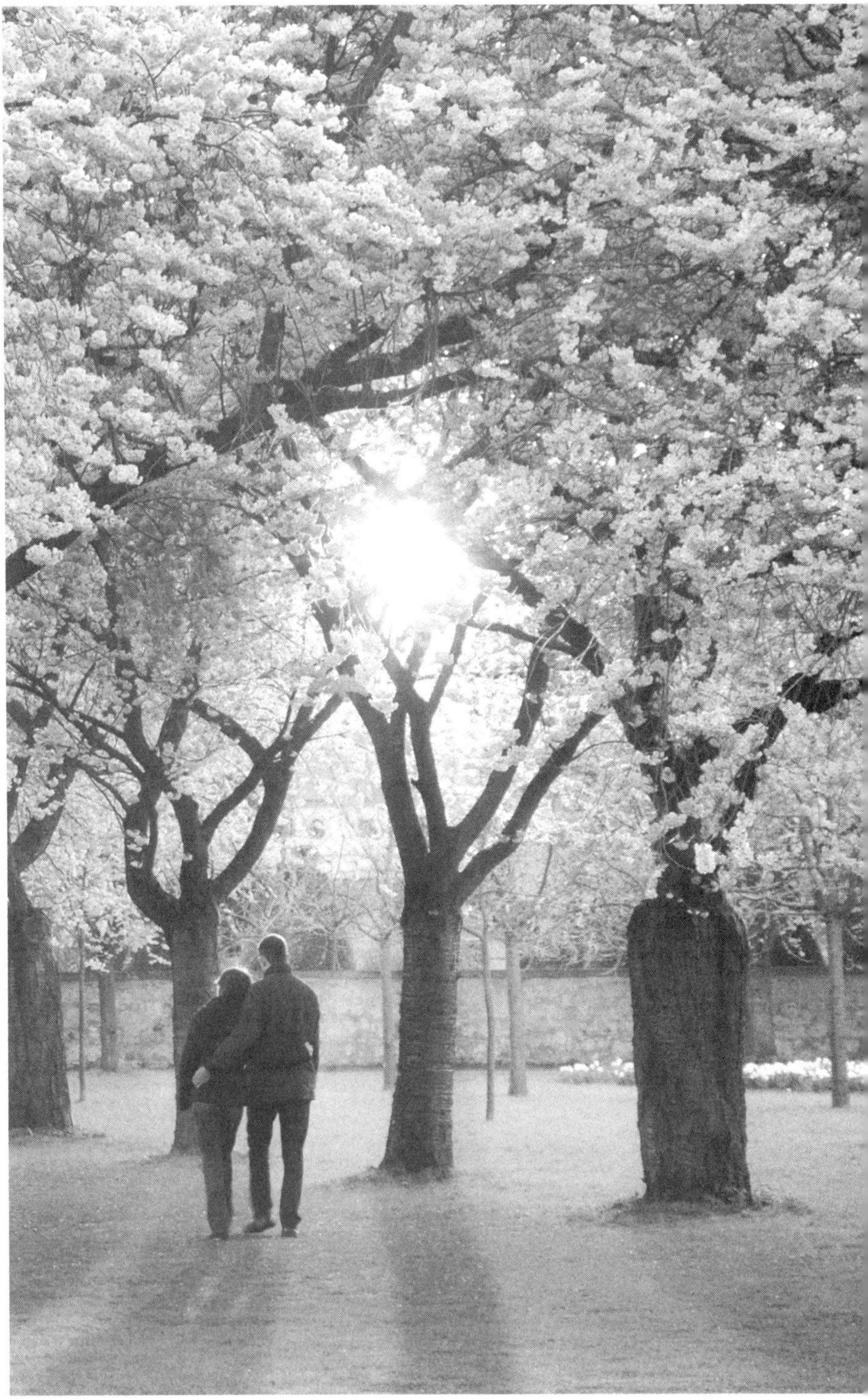

Conclusion

The challenge to live out these commandments in the context of our lives is, to say the least a forbidding proposition. The fact is that we could go down the list of all ten commandments and find that we have fallen short on each of them. Whether we apply these moral demands from God to marriage or to any other aspect of life, an honest assessment will show that we have missed the mark and fallen short of God's standard of perfection. Don't feel all alone in this condition because Romans 3:23 tells us that *"all have sinned and fallen short of the glory of God"* (NKJV).

The problem is compounded when we read that no one who has fallen short of God's standard will qualify to experience eternal life in His presence. Romans 6:23 says that the wages, or what we deserve for not meeting God's standard, is death. Death in the Bible refers to the separation from the love and mercy of God that we experience as sinners. When all of God's love and all of God's mercy is removed all that is left is pure torment and anguish. That is what the Bible describes as hell.

Every human being born into the world is facing that prospect for all eternity. God is a just Judge and so He cannot just wink at or excuse our sin. As a just Judge He is compelled to follow the law and to find us guilty on all ten counts. Those people who are banking on God simply understanding that they did the best they could, will be in for a rude awakening. It doesn't work in traffic court and it won't work before a just and righteous Judge.

There is hope however, because a strange thing happened in heaven long before we were born. God, being three Persons and yet one God, devised a plan that He would enter this world being born of a virgin. He would be the One man who would perfectly live out the commands of God as given in the Ten Commandments. After living a perfect life without sin He would go one step further and voluntarily take on Himself the punishment that we deserve for our sin. And that is exactly what happened. He literally experienced the grave and separation from the Father's love so that our sentence from the Judge would be fully satisfied. We committed the crime and He did our time! That is why we call it good news. It is good news for all of us who will confess that we need to take advantage of this salvation. It is good news for those of us who realize that God loves us and yet still has to judge rightly. It becomes good news as we personally accept this gift from the Saviour. It is not good news for anyone who neglects so great a salvation, for one day they will have to stand before that same Judge and hear the sentence rendered and have to pay the penalty for their sin themselves.

If you have fallen short in your marriage or if you have recognized that you have not lived up to God's perfect standard, then I implore you to take these few simple steps and receive forgiveness today. These four steps represent what God desires from all of us who have fallen short. They are simple, but not easy. They demand a change in our heart and an appreciation for what God has done for us by taking our place and tasting death so that we can have our record cleared with God. Here are the four steps:

Agree with God about your sin. The idea of confessing your sin is not to tell God what you did. He already knows what you did and doesn't need you to inform Him. The point of confession is to agree with God that your sin is as bad as He says it is. God desires that you stop making excuses and get on the same page with Him that your sin needs to stop. True confession leads to repentance, which is a turning away from the practice of your sin.

Acknowledge the historical events of the gospel story. In real time and space, in the city of Bethlehem, God was manifested in the flesh. He lived a sinless life as Jesus, and laid down His life on the cross at Calvary, as a substitutionary sacrifice for our sin. On the third day He rose bodily from the tomb, and was seen by hundreds of witnesses. After forty days He ascended back to the Father, where He sits today and makes intercession for believers.

Conclusion

Accept the free gift of salvation. I like to think of God's forgiveness as Christmas time. If I buy you a Christmas gift it would be an insult for you to reach into your pocket and try to pay for it. Especially if it is an expensive gift and all you have is a few coins. Imagine how God must feel after presenting us with the gift of His Son. Jesus was a gift that we could never deserve and could never pay for. Why would we ever think that we could do enough good to deserve such a gift? All we should do is say, Thank you, Jesus, and accept the gift without trying to earn it, deserve it, or pay God for it.

Allow God to be the Lord and director of your life. There are many people who come to Christ because they don't want to experience God's judgment. The problem is that God is not selling fire insurance. He wants you to experience a significant life as a part of the family of God. This is possible only as you accept Him as Lord as well as your Saviour. If you are accepting Jesus at all you have to accept Him for who He is. He is the King of the universe and will not be your servant or your genie in a bottle. He desires to sit on the throne of your heart and to direct your life.

You can take these four steps in prayer to God right now. The following prayer is an example of a prayer that includes these steps. Whether you pray these exact words or not, I encourage you to spend some time with God and with thanksgiving for His sacrificial death, asking Him for forgiveness and giving Him the control of your life.

Dear Lord Jesus, Thank You for making me and loving me, even when I've ignored You and gone my own way. I agree that I have sinned and fallen short of Your holy standard. I desire to turn from my sin and I ask You to forgive me. I need You in my life and I want to follow You from now on. Please come into my life and make me a new person inside. I accept Your gift of salvation. Please help me to grow now as a Christian.

But accepting God's forgiveness and help is not a magic wand. It does not mean that you will now perfectly live up to the Ten Commandments. However, accepting Christ is the first step on a long road to sanctification, to becoming the person

God wants you to be. With the help of the Holy Spirit you will change and be progressively conformed to the image of Jesus Christ. Rather than throwing your hands up in defeat by sin, you have the opportunity to experience increasing victory over sin in your life. My prayer is that you will come to know this victory over sin as you apply these commandments to your marriage and to your life.

Bibliography

"Your Greatest (true) Love Story" by Joan Smith, *Redbook* Oct. 2001 p. 98.

Sproul, R. C. *Discovering the intimate marriage*, Bethany Fellowship Inc. Minneapolis Minn. 1975

R. A. Schuller, *The world's greatest comebacks*, Thomas Nelson Publishers, Nashville TN 1988, pp. 158-159.

Meredith, Don, *Becoming One*, Thomas Nelson Publishers, Nashville TN

Mason, M., *The Mystery of Marriage*, Multnomah Press, Portland OR, 1953

Gilder, G., *Men and marriage*. Pelican Publishing Co. Gretna LA. 1986

Emphasis, Sept/Oct, 2001, p. 15.

Also by Dr. Tony Hart:

Winning is Everything

"Enjoyable, inspiring, profitable, and immensely encouraging—here is a book that everyone can enjoy. Tony Hart does an excellent job to lift up one's spirits in the midst of troubles. The book is well-illustrated, easy to read, and you won't want to put it down."

Alexander Strauch
Author of Biblical Eldership

Tony Hart addresses the issue of the victorious Christian life. Using the book of Numbers from the Old Testament as the foundation for his exposition, Tony reveals how the spiritual victories received by the saints of old can be ours today. He shows us how God desires to lead us, provide for us, protect us, and strengthen us in the midst of various situations.

With contemporary illustrations, clear Biblical exposition and in the common man's language, Dr. Tony Hart helps us to experientially know what it means to be more than conquerors in Christ and how we can more seriously accept our responsibility to remain faithful to God's Word, while courageously preventing the enemy's plan from governing our lives.

May God richly bless you as you read and apply these practical truths from God's Word.

from the forward by Dr. Tony Evans
Senior Pastor - Oak Cliff Bible Fellowship
President - Urban Alternative